ACCEPTED IN THE FATHER'S LOVE

*Removing all religious burdens through
the knowledge of the finished work of Jesus Christ*

MATHEW SIMON

Copyright © 2017 by Mathew Simon

Accepted In The Father's Love
Removing all religious burdens through the knowledge of the finished work of Jesus Christ
by Mathew Simon

Printed in the United States of America.

ISBN 9781498497053

All rights reserved solely by the author. The author guarantees all contents are original and do not infringe upon the legal rights of any other person or work. No part of this book may be reproduced in any form without the permission of the author. The views expressed in this book are not necessarily those of the publisher.

Unless otherwise indicated, Scripture quotations taken from the Word English Bible version of the Bible. This is a Public Domain Bible (no copyright) modern English translation of the Holy Bible based on the American Standard Version.

Scripture quotations taken from the Holy Bible, New International Version (NIV). Copyright © 1973, 1978, 1984 by Zondervan Publishing House. Used by permission. All rights reserved.

Scripture quotations taken from the New American Standard Bible (NASB). Copyright © 1960, 1962, 1963, 1968, 1971, 1972, 1973, 1975, 1977, 1995 by The Lockman Foundation. Used by permission. All rights reserved.

Scripture quotations taken from the Holy Bible, New Living Translation (NLT). Copyright ©1996, 2004, 2007 by Tyndale House Foundation. Used by permission of Tyndale House Publishers, Inc.

Scripture quotations taken from the King James Version (KJV) – *public domain.*

In some Scripture quotes, the author has marked certain words in bold or upper case to enforce certain points of discussion.

www.xulonpress.com

Contents

Dedication vii

Introduction ix

Chapter 1 My story 11

Chapter 2 New covenant 19

Chapter 3 End times are over 36

Chapter 4 No more fear 65

Chapter 5 Jesus has finished the work 91

Chapter 6 Faith of Christ 100

Chapter 7 Universal salvation 116

Chapter 8 Free from religious rules 131

Chapter 9 God loves you 165

About the Author 183

Acknowledgments 185

Dedication

This book is dedicated to my loving wife and our three wonderful children. You are God's biggest blessings in my life.

This writing is also dedicated to people all over the world who have been burdened by the heavy expectations of religion.

I hope and pray that this book may reveal to you just how much God your Father loves you.

Introduction

The greatest need for all people is to know that God loves them. As I have experienced the Christian faith, I have realized that this knowledge of God is based on our understanding of the Bible. If we misunderstand the context, then we can be burdened with religious fear and compulsion. But if we know the truth, it will set us free to enjoy the Father's love.

In this book, I would like to describe my journey in knowing the love of God. My hope for all of us is simply described here:

Ephesians 3:19 "to know Christ's love which surpasses knowledge"

Chapter 1

My Story

When I look back at my life, I never imagined that I would write any book, especially a book about Jesus. I was the last person who would have any interest in the Bible. I was born as the youngest of three children to an Indian family living in Kuwait. We were not regular Churchgoers for various reasons, but mainly because my father did not like religion too much. He believed in Jesus but did not like the Church's constant requests for money. He preferred to personally help the poor instead of funding buildings and Church activities. My Dad was always very loving and kind to me. His love and care for me were a taste of heaven on earth because later in life, I realized that this is how our Heavenly Father loves us.

I spent most of my childhood not knowing too much about God except for our annual Church visits on Christmas and Easter. All I remember was that the services were long and uninteresting and I could barely understand anything. When I grew older, my mother sent me to VBS (Vacation Bible School) during our summer holidays. She also taught me how to pray to God, although I rarely prayed at that time. A few years later I was prepared to officially become a Christian. We were all baptized as infants in our Church, but after the age of 12, we were invited to accept Jesus as our Lord and Savior. In those days, we were shown the "Jesus movie" so that we could understand the Gospel. To be honest, I don't remember much except that we were told that we had to surrender our lives to Jesus and make Him Lord. It sounded too complicated and terrifying, to be honest. I wasn't sure what I was doing, but I stood up and accepted Jesus because everyone else was doing it.

Knowing God for the first time

A few months later, our lives were rocked. While we were on vacation in India in 1990, the Iraqi army invaded my adopted homeland of Kuwait. I had to forcibly continue my High School education in India, but this turned out to be a blessing in disguise. It helped me enroll into one of the good universities in India as a student of Computer Science. For the first time, I left home to live away from my parents. I was struggling with my studies, and I had failed in Math and Chemistry. It was the first time in my life that something like this had happened. I had to retake the exams during the winter holidays and miss out on going back home to my family. It was one of the lowest points in my life, and I started praying to God for the first time. In His great mercy and kindness, He overturned the results due to an error in the way they had examined my original scores. I could enjoy my holidays at home and my life completely changed. Later on, I graduated from College with good scores and got a job. At that time, I knew the love of God even though I was not going to Church, except for my occasional trips to the local Catholic Church. I had no knowledge of sin or works or even faith. I just prayed to God whenever I needed help, and He always answered. I had no fear in life in spite of the challenges of college and beginning a career. Later on, God helped me get a job in America as a Software Engineer.

My introduction to the Bible

After I got married in 1999, we were living in Northern California as a young couple. We started going to Church more often, but I still had no knowledge of the Bible. Going to Church was more of a tradition than anything else. But everything changed in 2001. After I had lost my job due to the economic crisis, the next shock was the tragedy of 9/11. This horrific event was considered by many in the Christian world as a sign of the end times. As a child, I had heard that we were living in the end times and knew about the prophecies of Nostradamus. The events of 9/11 ignited my passion to know more about the end times, the antichrist, 2nd coming of Christ, etc. I started reading the Bible and searching the Internet about these topics. In the following months, I learned that Jesus was returning in the end times and that we all needed to be ready. For the first time in my life, I found a Gospel tract on the Internet. I was told that I was a sinner going to hell and that I had to confess my sins and believe in Jesus to go to heaven. Till now, I was never aware of my sins with respect to God because I had only related to Him by simple faith. It was a bit like Adam who did not know good or evil but only knew the Father's love. From that time onwards I became conscious of my sins. There began my journey into the system of organized religion. After a few months as I listened to a Christian song, I was consumed with the awareness that Jesus had forgiven my sins and I was so thankful to Him. This was my first salvation experience – the first of many, during the last 15 years. Over the next few years, I had a great appetite for the Bible and was learning about the New Testament. We became a lot more active in Church and joined a Bible study fellowship.

Stop sinning because Jesus is coming

As I studied the Bible, the awareness of my sins grew strongly, and I started feeling a lot more convicted of many small sins which I had never even bothered about before. I started going to a Charismatic prayer group where they were all speaking in tongues, and it made me very curious and hungry for the spiritual gifts. It was at that time that I was introduced to the concept of having a "quiet time" of prayer with the Lord. At that time, I listened to many preachers who would preach a lot about holiness, repentance and obeying Jesus, especially in keeping the Ten Commandments in heart, word and deed. As the months passed by, I would spend almost two hours a day praying to the Lord, confessing my sins, repenting and asking Him to speak to me. He would show me many scriptures where it said that He was coming soon to judge the world.

I asked the Lord what to do, and I would see scriptures where I had to deny myself and carry the cross. I gave Gospel tracts and witnessed to strangers telling them to repent because Jesus was coming soon. I made videos on YouTube and sent urgent warnings to all my Christian friends. I preached that they had to repent and be baptized for their sins and forsake their infant baptism. I warned them to stop sinning because we had to be holy and ready for Christ's 2nd coming. I preached heavily on repentance, confession and carrying the cross. Every Sunday I would stand in line for the Lord's Supper, confessing every known sin in thought, word and deed. At times, I would be crying in great remorse over my pride, anger and bitterness at others. One day I thought the Holy Spirit told me to call up and apologize to people whom I had hurt many years ago. To my surprise, many of them did not even remember my sins. All these were my attempts at restitution for past sins. I would pray to the Lord to help me be holy and stop sinning. I would confess my sins every time I sinned in thought, word or attitude. During the day at the office, I would run from my desk into my car, crying out to God to forgive me because I entertained an angry thought at my coworker.

As I was trying to become a disciple of Jesus Christ, I learned from the Bible that He had commanded all His disciples to sell all their possessions and preach the Gospel. I was prepared to sell our home and move into an apartment so that I could preach this fire and brimstone Gospel to the world. Thankfully, my wife shot that idea down and instilled common sense into me. But I was still zealously trying to follow Jesus. The next step was to be baptized in the Holy Spirit. I would pray for hours and spend days in fasting, hoping to receive the gift of speaking in tongues. I asked several people to pray and lay hands on me, but nothing happened. Someone once told me to pray for others, and yet it did not come. I was desperate to be filled with the Spirit. After taking the water baptism in obedience to Acts 2:38, I spent an entire week in fasting. But at the end of the week, it was my wife who was filled with the Spirit, speaking in tongues. The funny thing was that she never even fasted or prayed much for it. I was the one who fasted, prayed and was following Jesus by carrying the cross. It was a big blow, and the sheer intensity of my Christian walk was taking a toll on me.

From Grace into the Mixed Gospel

At that time, I started reading the book of Romans and Galatians again and began to realize that I was saved by grace and not my efforts of confession, repentance or carrying any cross. I distinctly remember the Lord telling me one day, "I carried the cross for you so that you don't have to". A weight lifted off my shoulder as I stopped striving and began resting in the grace of God. Over the next two years, God gave me a lot of opportunities to preach the Gospel of Grace. I was at a lot of peace and was enjoying my Christian life again. But inevitably, I slipped back into works and confession of sins once again. But this time it was a deadly mixture. In the past, I used to believe in works-based salvation but now it was a mixed Gospel. Now I believed in salvation by grace but that I could also lose this salvation if I did not forgive others. I used to sincerely recite the Lord's Prayer meaning every word from the bottom of my heart. I tried to forgive others so that God would forgive me. But there was a certain person I could never forgive no matter how hard I tried. I became fearful and unsure of my salvation. At that time, I faced a lot of problems at my job. Over the previous five years, I was very successful in my career and was one of the top employees in my team. But due to some unforeseen circumstances, I had to change jobs and was under tremendous stress. I was stuck in a job that I hated. I could not find a good job, and I thought that God was testing my faith. A few months later, I fell into depression. I thought my life was doomed to doing something I hated because God was forcing me to surrender my desires and carry the cross. The truth is that Jesus told the Jews that they could not mix the Old Covenant Law and the New Covenant Grace because it was like mixing new wine in old wineskins. When we mix the grace of God with the threats of losing salvation, then the result is defeat and despair. As a result, I had lost all interest in preaching or teaching the Bible.

At that time, God would go out of His way to speak to me through the Bible and other special signs. He would show me that He is making all things new (Revelation 21:5) although I would only understand this truth later. I was still consumed with depression and sadness. There was one time when I had played video games one night without praying or reading the Bible. The next morning I woke up with guilty thoughts about it. As I was cooking breakfast, I accidentally burnt my finger. I thought that God was punishing me because I had not read the Bible in the previous night. I was sad that I was unable to play video games with my burnt finger. But a few minutes later, I found a Bible verse lying on the table. It was Jeremiah 29:11, where God promised good and prosperous plans for me. I just started thanking God for His love and noticed that my finger was healed completely without me asking for it. A few days later, God showed me this verse.

John 16:20 "Most certainly I tell you, that you will weep and lament, but the world will rejoice. You will be sorrowful, but your sorrow will be turned into joy."

Not to soon after that day, my wife prayed to the Lord, and He confirmed to her that He would give me the desire of my heart.

Psalm 20:4 NLT "May he grant your heart's desires and make all your plans succeed"

He gave me this glorious assurance that His love for me was not based on what job I took or what I did in life. I did not have to surrender my desires to please Him, but that He was with me wherever I went and whatever I did.

Joshua 1:9 "Be strong and courageous! Do not tremble or be dismayed, for the LORD your God is with you wherever you go."

I faced a lot of challenges in my new job and went through great fear and distress, but God never allowed anything bad happen to me. He miraculously protected me. This was not because of my faith that was at rock bottom anyway but only because of His love and grace that carried me.

Isaiah 43:2-3 NLT "When you go through deep waters, I will be with you. When you go through rivers of difficulty, you will not drown. When you walk through the fire of oppression, you will not be burned up; the flames will not consume you. For I am the LORD, your God"

Righteousness by Grace

I was healed of depression instantly when I finally believed that God had made me righteous apart from my works. I realized that I was already righteous in Christ without surrendering my career or desires. It was at that time that God introduced me to the teachings of many preachers of grace. For the next two years, I was established in the righteousness of faith and grace without my works. Joy and peace were finally restored to my life. I also started praying in tongues when I stopped trying to attain it by my efforts. It happened when I realized that the Holy Spirit was already living in me and that there was no more striving but simply exercising it in faith. I also started being a lot more confident in my walk with the Lord. We started experiencing healing by believing that we were healed by the stripes of Jesus on the cross. We believed that Christ became poor for us to become rich. The prosperity Gospel was a great blessing after I was coming out of depression. I was walking in the word of faith, confessing verses, declaring that I was righteous and blessed in Christ. I was also commanding mountains to move and rebuking Satan for every hindrance ranging from traffic jams to problems at work. I did notice some success in overcoming these problems, but it did not always happen. I remember one funny incident when I was down with the flu and no amount of believing and confessing verses could get me healed. But I continued to believe in God's promises of restoration because of what Jesus did on the cross.

Zechariah 9:11-12 "As for you also, because of the blood of your covenant ... even today I declare that I will restore double to you."

Joel 2:24 "The threshing floors will be full of wheat, and the vats will overflow with new wine and oil. I will restore to you the years that the swarming locust has eaten"

God was restoring all the years I had lost when I was under Old Covenant thinking. He was bringing me back to the New Covenant of Grace and peace. I started teaching about the righteousness of grace to all my friends, and it was blessing many people. God had restored my teaching ministry.

From Grace into the fulfilled End Times

At that time, I began my ministry on Facebook and started writing a blog. God began to take me on a very exciting journey of connecting with people all over the world and ministering the Gospel of grace, as He promised to me a few months ago. It was at that time when He started revealing a greater grace than I ever knew before. It was the revelation of the fact that the end times were over in the year 70AD. In the past, we have seen many failed predictions of the rapture. But now, God was showing me through the scriptures, that the 2nd coming of Christ had already happened. It was not a world-ending event, but it was a Covenant-ending event. It was the end of the Old Covenant through the destruction of Jerusalem in 70AD. As I started prayerfully studying the Bible, God repeatedly confirmed this truth to me. I began teaching this truth, and it set many people free all over the world. It gave me new hope and optimism for life on earth. The world was not going to end.

God's universal love and salvation

There was, however, this nagging feeling in my mind. What about hell and the fate of unbelievers, if the second coming of Christ and the judgment has already happened? From my experience, if unbelievers had troubled me, I would secretly hope they were going to hell. But God was changing my mind. He had never intended to roast His creation in an eternal fire. The words "hell" and "lake of fire" were simply symbolic names for the destruction of Jerusalem and the Old Covenant system in 70AD. This revelation made me understand the Father's heart of love and grace in a way like never before. I was glad to know that unbelievers would not be burnt forever, but that they would just perish or cease to exist after death.

That was when God powerfully changed my world in 2016. Through a series of circumstances and studying the scriptures, I found out that God is so good, that He saves all people even after death. This coincided with my struggles of faith in God's promise of restoring my career. I would believe, confess verses and stand on God's promises but nothing was happening. I would go through religious mood swings. On some days, I would be praising God for His reassurance, and on other days I would be shaking my fist in anger at Him due to the delays. Despite all of this, He kept telling me that He found no flaw in me and that I was His beloved son. I finally came to realize that God's promises were not based on my faith, but on His faithfulness. I did not have to struggle to make it happen because it was based on the faith of Christ. This revelation has brought even greater peace and rest to my life because I no longer had to depend on my faith. My Father was taking care of my life based on His love and not my faith. This was when He showed me clearly in the Bible that He has saved all humanity by making a New Covenant where He does not account sin anymore, not even the sin of unbelief.

Matthew 11:29 "Come to me, all you who labor and are heavily burdened, and I will give you rest."

I was set free from all religious works and was at complete rest knowing that I did not have to do anything anymore. I started seeing the love of God in all my friends, in both unbelievers and believers. Life has become beautiful where I just enjoy all the gifts of family, food, drink, hobbies and every simple pleasure of life, knowing that God loves everyone in the world.

Christ has done everything

Philippians 3:4,7-8 "Though I myself might have confidence even in the flesh. If any other man thinks that he has confidence in the flesh, I yet more ... However, I consider those things that were gain to me as a loss for Christ. Yes most certainly, and I count all things to be a loss for the excellency of the knowledge of Christ Jesus"

When I look back at my life, there was probably not one of my peers, who prayed, fasted, believed, confessed, repented and did all the religious works more than I did. I took every word of the Bible as seriously as I could but finally realized that Jesus is the One whose obedience made me righteous. I don't boast in all my efforts anymore because I consider it nothing compared to knowing Jesus who did everything for me.

Revelation 21:6 NASB "I will give to the one who thirsts from the spring of the water of life without cost."

I could only understand grace after going through the parched desert of self-righteousness and religion. After running on the treadmill of religious self-efforts like faith, works, confession and repentance, I was finally put to rest by realizing that the rivers of living water were always within me. He was already living in me, without any of my efforts.

*John 7:38 "from **within** him will flow rivers of living water"*

I did not have to do anything because Christ had already done everything. God had already chosen me before I was even born to proclaim Jesus Christ who lives in us.

*Galatians 1:15-16 "But when it was the good pleasure of God, who separated me from my mother's womb, and called me through his grace, **to reveal his Son in me**, that I might preach him"*

God has finally fulfilled the desire of my heart to write to you about Jesus who lives in every one of us. A lot of what I mentioned in this chapter will be explained in greater detail in the rest of the book. I hope you enjoy the ride.

Chapter 2

New Covenant

*I*n the beginning, it was so good. God created Adam & Eve, and they were enjoying life in the garden, eating & drinking happily and ruling over the earth. Adam was the son of God (Luke 3:38), and God was walking with him. It was simply Daddy and His kids enjoying life together.

The Old Creation

When God made all things good, it was not a perfect physical experience. Adam was not floating on wings or free of the common cold. He was made in flesh and blood that would not last forever and therefore he was not perfect in behavior. I'm sure he had arguments with Eve over which food to eat for dinner. But he was made in God's image having His Spirit/breath, and he was perfectly righteous in his own eyes. Adam had absolutely no knowledge of good or evil or any religious works, but only knew the love of the Father. He had zero sin-consciousness, and that is why he did not know that he was naked. His physical nakedness was a symbol of spiritual nakedness because God told him that he would spiritually "die" on the very day he ate from the tree by knowing that he was naked. The knowledge of good and evil instantly killed him.

Genesis 2:16-17 NIV "The Lord God commanded the man, saying, "From any tree of the garden you may eat freely; but from the tree of the knowledge of good and evil you shall not eat, for in the day that you eat from it you will surely die."

We know that it was the "serpent" that tempted Eve to become like God when she was already made in His image. Humanity was already righteous by grace, but the temptation was to attain it by being good and avoiding evil. This tree was the symbol of the Ten Commandments that was given to Israel many years later. How do we know that? It was the law that made the Jews conscious of sin and killed them spiritually.

*Romans 3:20 "For through the law comes the **knowledge of sin**"*

*Romans 7:7,9 "I wouldn't have known sin, except through the law. For I wouldn't have known coveting, unless the law had said, "You shall not covet. ...... I was alive apart from the law once, but when the commandment came, sin revived, and **I died**"*

The law was the full manifestation of the tree of knowledge of good and evil. So, when Adam & Eve ate, they died spiritually, and not physically. They instantly realized their spiritual nakedness and were afraid of God. This was the beginning of the "Old Creation" which began to die spiritually till the ministry of death came to Israel through the Ten Commandments (2nd Corinthians 3:7-9). But God was so good that He already prepared the solution. He instantly clothed Adam with the skin of the animal that was pointing to Christ's future sacrifice. This was because Christ Himself covered their nakedness.

Galatians 3:27 NIV "for all of you who were baptized into Christ have clothed yourselves with Christ"

Isaiah 61:10 "for he has clothed me with the garments of salvation. He has covered me with the robe of righteousness."

Adam received the curse of sweat and fruitless labor. God never cursed him, but the system of good & evil did this to him. Jesus would come later and pour out His blood through his sweat in the garden of Gethsemane to reverse the curse (Luke 22:44). His labor on the cross was fruitful because He saved us. Adam blamed Eve for his sin, but Christ made us His bride, to become holy and blameless by giving up His life.

Ephesians 5:25-27 NIV "Christ loved the church and gave himself up for her to make her holy, cleansing her by the washing with water through the word, and to present her to himself as a radiant church, without stain or wrinkle or any other blemish, but holy and <u>blameless</u>."

1st Timothy 2:15 "but she will be saved through her childbearing"

Eve faced the prospect of painful childbirth, but God told Eve t̃ would be saved by her descendant, Jesus Christ who would crush the ser̃ pent's head by destroying the Law. Adam & Eve who tried to become wise by eating the fruit, lost God's righteousness until Christ freely gave us His wisdom and the gift of His righteousness (1st Corinthians 1:30).

The shadows pointed to Christ

One of the common messages I have heard from well-meaning preachers is that God is calling us like Abraham or He has chosen us like Moses. We are told to look at the faith of David, Daniel or Job. Now, they were great men of faith, but they were not the real deal. They were all journeying in faith till the reality of Christ was revealed. Our identity is found in Christ in whom we have been made sons of God. They were all servants of God, but we are Sons of the Father. We are told to be under the Ten Commandments or tithing, but the reality is found in Christ and not in rules. **Every story in the Bible pointed to Jesus.**

Colossians 2:17 NIV "These are a shadow of the things that were to come; the reality, however, is found in Christ"

When Abel made the sacrifice and died at the hands of Cain, it was pointing to Christ's death at the hands of religion. When Enoch was caught up to God, it was a sign of Christ lifting up all people and seating us in heavenly places. When Noah entered the ark with his family, it was a sign of Christ taking all of us into the presence of God. When Abraham gave up his son Isaac, it was a picture of the Father giving up His only Son, Jesus for the world. When Isaac married Rebekah, it was a shadow of Christ marrying His bride, the Church. When Joseph was betrayed by his brothers, it was about Christ being crucified by His countrymen. When Joseph was the king who saved those same brothers from the famine, it was a picture of Christ saving the world from spiritual death. When Moses led the Jews out of Egypt across the Red Sea, it was a picture of Christ saving all men. When Joshua led the Jews into the promised land of Canaan, it was a picture of Yeshua (Jesus) taking us into the promised land of salvation. When David was appointed as king, it was Christ who was the true king of kings! When Solomon brought peace, wealth and wisdom to Israel, it was Christ who was our true wisdom, shalom and wealth. When God called Israel as His son whom He called out of Egypt in Hosea 11:1, it was fulfilled when Christ returned from Egypt after being hidden there from Herod (Matt 2:13). The last prophet and greatest man under the Law was John the Baptist, whose only task was to point Israel to the Son of God, Jesus Christ!

This is why we don't try to insert ourselves into the Bible but see that God has placed us into Christ. We are not trying to be perfect like all those wonderful Bible characters, but Christ is our reality who has made us perfect. Jesus is our righteousness, and He has finished the work for us.

Christ gave grace to those under the Law

When the Ten Commandments were given on Sinai, it was not God's will for the Israelites to be condemned. The Israelites were the ones who demanded the Law by boasting that they could obey everything (Exodus 19:8) instead of just relying on the grace of God that carried them out of Egypt. It was similar to the self-righteousness of Adam who thought he could become like God by knowing good and evil, instead of resting in the position of sonship by knowing the Father's love.

Romans 3:19-20 "under the law, that every mouth may be closed, and all the world may be brought under the judgment of God. Because by the works of the law, no flesh will be justified in his sight. For through the law comes the knowledge of sin."

Under the Old Covenant, the Jews represented all of humanity as the high priests, but this covenant made all men guilty. The Law was given to shut the mouths of men so that sin may increase and they would stop trusting in their self-righteousness.

The Law was the ministry of death and condemnation because the Jews who trusted in the Law received the wages of death. Sin was to be "under the Law". It was not talking about "sins" as in actions, but to be under the system of self-righteousness.

Romans 4:4 NIV "Now to the one who works, wages are not credited as a gift but as an obligation."

The Jews who worked under this system of "do good and avoid evil" would receive wages based on their performance. They would be judged by their actions. The wage was spiritual death because nobody could become righteous by keeping the Law.

Romans 6:23 "For the wages of sin is death, but the free gift of God is eternal life in Christ Jesus our Lord."

But God gave the gift of salvation through Jesus Christ. Just like the Ten Commandments was the full manifestation of the tree of knowledge of good & evil that brought spiritual death, now Jesus Christ is the full manifestation of the tree of life that brought salvation. This gift was not given to those who worked for it, but freely to the ungodly! God had made humanity righteous through the death and resurrection of Christ. It was completely His work and not man's effort!

Romans 4:5,7-8,24-25 NIV "However, to the one who does not work but trusts God who justifies the ungodly, their faith is credited as righteousness. ... Blessed are those whose transgressions are forgiven, whose sins are covered. Blessed is the one whose sin the Lord will never count against them. ...... God will credit righteousness – for us who believe in him who raised Jesus our Lord from the dead. He was delivered over to death for our sins and was raised to life for our justification"

But the Jews tried to attain righteousness by trusting in the Law. The Pharisees taught them to be righteous by circumcision, tithing and keeping the Ten Commandments superficially. Their self-righteousness had to be broken. Otherwise, they would perish in unbelief. This is why Christ told them to attain perfection in the Sermon on the Mount. He told them to they could not be saved unless their righteousness far exceeded that of the Pharisees (Matthew 5:20). To the Jews who thought they could be righteous by avoiding adultery, Christ told them that lust would condemn them. If they thought they could be righteous by avoiding murder, He told them to cut out anger to escape judgment. If they assumed that they could attain salvation by circumcision, then He told them to cut off the hand and eye that sinned. If they thought they could keep the Law by only loving their brothers, then Jesus told them to fulfill the Law and be as perfect as God, by loving their enemies. He told them that if they wanted to see God, then they would have to become pure in heart. In one sermon, Jesus completely shattered their self-righteousness of keeping the Ten Commandments. The Jews failed to keep the Law because they could not love God with all their heart, soul and strength.

The Good News is that Christ made all of humanity righteous apart from the Ten Commandments and ceremonial laws.

*Romans 3:21-24 "But now apart from the law, a righteousness of God has been revealed, being testified by the law and the prophets; even the righteousness of God through faith in Jesus Christ **to all and on all those who believe**. For there is no distinction, for all have sinned, and fall short of the glory of God; being **justified freely by his grace** through the redemption that is in Christ Jesus"*

All were guilty under the Law, no matter how good or bad they performed. But all were made righteous in Christ – both Jew and Gentile. All were justified freely by grace. It was not just those who believed, but even all of humanity. Both pastor and prisoner are righteous in Christ. Under the Law, only those who were pure & sinless in heart could see God, and that disqualified everyone. But now, everyone who believed in Christ has seen the Father and is pure in heart. This was pure grace!

*John 14:9 "He who has **seen** me has **seen** the **Father**"*

*Acts 15:9 NIV "He did not discriminate between us and them, for **he purified their hearts** by faith"*

Salvation from the wrath of the Law

Romans 4:15 "the law produces wrath"

The Jews didn't want grace but preferred to trust in the Law instead. They were blind to the fact that the Law brought a curse and wrath on those who trusted in it (Galatians 3:10). John the Baptist told the Pharisees that this wrath was coming upon their generation.

Matthew 3:7 "But when he saw many of the Pharisees and Sadducees coming for his baptism, he said to them, "You offspring of vipers, who warned you to flee from the wrath to come?"

The Jews had crucified Christ and were persecuting the believers all over the Roman Empire for 40 years. The wrath upon them was about to happen very soon.

*1st Thessalonians 2:15-16 "**the Jews who killed the Lord Jesus** and the prophets and also drove us out. They displease God and are hostile to everyone in their effort to keep us from speaking to the Gentiles so that they may be saved. In this way they always heap up their sins to the limit. **The wrath of God has come upon them AT LAST.**"*

The curse of the Law was coming upon the land of Israel as prophesied by the prophet Malachi, in the last book of the Old Testament. John the Baptist announced the immediate fulfillment of this prophecy in Matthew 3:10 when he said that the Pharisees would be cast into the fire of destruction.

*Malachi 4:1,6 NIV "Surely the day is coming; it will burn like a furnace. All the arrogant and every evildoer will be stubble, and the day that is coming will set them on fire, ... I will come and strike the **land** with total destruction."*

The Roman armies destroyed the land of Israel in the year 70AD. That was the time when the wrath of the Law was poured out on Israel. All things in the Bible were fulfilled at that time.

*Luke 21:20-23 "But **when you see Jerusalem surrounded by armies**, then know that its desolation is at hand. Then let those who are in Judea flee to the mountains. Let those who are in the middle of her depart. Let those who are in the country not enter therein. For these are days of vengeance, that **all things which are written may be fulfilled**. Woe to those who are pregnant and to those who nurse infants in those days! For there will be great **distress in the land, and wrath to this people**."*

The believers, who trusted in Jesus, were saved from this wrath by fleeing from Jerusalem before it was destroyed in 70AD.

*Romans 5:9-10 "God commends his own love toward us, in that while we were yet sinners, Christ died for us. Much more then, being now **justified** by his blood, we will be **saved from God's wrath through him**. For if, while we were enemies, we were reconciled to God through the death of his Son, much more, being reconciled, we will be saved **by his life**."*

These Jewish 1st Century believers were previously under the Law. In the past, Israel had voluntarily become the enemies of God by choosing the Law on Sinai instead of trusting in His grace. It was a war that man started against God. They made Him their judge instead of their provider. God was never angry with them and never wanted to put them under the Law and its wrath. God is love, and He demonstrated it to the Jews that Christ died for them while they were sinners. Those who believed the words of Christ were saved from the wrath when they escaped the destruction that came upon the Jewish Old Covenant system in Jerusalem and throughout the Roman Empire in 70AD.

Transition from Old to New Covenant

Over the last 15 years, one of the most fascinating things I have learned in the Bible is about the covenants. We know that the New Covenant of forgiveness began with the death of Christ on the cross. Christ had died for the sins committed under the Old Covenant because it was the Law that imputed sins to the Jews.

Hebrews 9:15 NIV "Christ is the mediator of a new covenant, that those who are called may receive the promised eternal inheritance – now that he has died as a ransom to set them free from the sins committed under the first covenant."

But what is unknown to many people is that the Old Covenant did not end on the Cross but only passed away in 70AD.

*Hebrews 8:13 NLT "When God speaks of a "new" covenant, it means he has made the first one obsolete. It is now out of date and will **soon** disappear."*

In Hebrews 10:9, we know that Christ came to set aside the Old Covenant and to make a New Covenant. But the New Covenant was not fully revealed as long as the Temple and the sacrifices remained in Jerusalem, at the time when the Bible was written.

Hebrews 9:8-9 NIV "The Holy Spirit was showing by this that the way into the Most Holy Place had not yet been disclosed as long as the first tabernacle was still functioning. This is an illustration for the PRESENT TIME"

In 70AD, the Temple of Jerusalem was destroyed. It was at that time that the ministry and persecution of the Pharisees ended. That was when the Old Covenant passed away.

The Jewish believers were eagerly waiting for this salvation from the wrath. They were waiting for the removal of the Old Covenant when their sins would finally be abolished. They were eagerly waiting for Christ's second coming to destroy the Temple and bring an end to the Old Covenant in 70AD.

*Hebrews 9:28 "Christ also, having been offered once to bear the sins of many, will appear a second time, without sin, to those who are **eagerly** waiting for him for **salvation**."*

They had obeyed Christ and endured the persecution and tribulation to be saved in the end (Matthew 24). He would not delay His coming anymore because He promised He was returning soon to establish the New Covenant.

Hebrews 10:37 "In a VERY LITTLE WHILE, he who COMES will come, and will NOT WAIT."

Revelation 22:20 "He who TESTIFIES these things says, "Yes, I come QUICKLY."

This is why the Jews were told to leave the city of Jerusalem and follow Jesus in spite of the persecution from the Pharisees.

Hebrews 13:12-14 NIV "Jesus also suffered outside the city gate to make the people holy through his own blood. Let us, then, go to him outside the camp, bearing the disgrace he bore. For here we do not have an enduring city, but we are looking for the city that is to come."

The physical city of Jerusalem was destroyed in 70AD, and the enduring spiritual city of the New Jerusalem was revealed.

Romans 11:26-27 "so all Israel will be saved. Even as it is written, "There will come out of Zion the Deliverer, and he will turn away ungodliness from Jacob. This is my covenant to them, when I will take away their sins."

In 70AD, the Old Covenant came to an end. That was the time of the final judgment and wrath upon those who trusted in the Law. It was the time of salvation for those who believed. At that time the wrath was finished, and a New Covenant was made where the sins of the Law were taken away forever and ever.

Revelation 15:1 "God's wrath is finished"

Old Heaven and Earth (Old Covenant) vs. New Heaven and Earth (New Covenant)

Some of us say that the Ten Commandments still applies to the world today but that the ceremonial law of Moses has passed away. But Christ told the Jews in Matthew 5:18, that not even the slightest part of the Law be removed until heaven and earth passed away. If that is the case, then we better pack our bags and fly off to Jerusalem, get circumcised and offer sacrifices. Obviously, that is not true, and most Christians do not believe in keeping the ceremonial laws. So then what was the passing away of the "heaven and earth" that would take away the Law and fulfill all things as Christ said in Matthew 24:35? We will find that the "heaven and earth" was the Law of Moses that testified against the sins of the Jews.

*Deuteronomy 31:26,29 NIV "Take this **Book of the Law** and place it beside the ark of the covenant of the* LORD *your God. **There it will remain as a witness** against you ......**the heavens and the earth to testify** against them"*

In the original language of the Jews, their "heaven and earth" was their Law, Priesthood and Temple. It was the system of the Old Covenant. Several scriptures prove that the "heaven and earth" was Israel and the temple in Jerusalem (Psalm 50:4, Ezra 5:11, Joel 3:16). It was the presence of God on earth, which separated the Jews from the Gentiles. In the Old Testament, we will find that the shaking of the "heaven and earth" was the destruction of the Temple by the Babylonians. After the exile, the Jews returned to restore the Temple again.

Haggai 2:6, 15 NIV "In a little while I will once more shake the heavens and the earth...consider how things were before one stone was laid on another in the L{\sc ord}'s temple"

The Jews created the old heaven on earth by building the Temple, laying one stone upon another. But Jesus told the disciples that they would witness the end of the old heaven and earth when the Temple was destroyed, and not one stone would remain on another (Matthew 24:2). At that time, the Hebrew believers in Christ were receiving the kingdom of God when the "old heaven and earth" was destroyed.

Hebrews 12:26-28 NIV "Now he has promised, saying, "Yet once more I will shake not only the earth, but also the heavens." This phrase, "Yet once more", signifies the removing of those things that are shaken, as of things that have been made, that those things which are not shaken may remain. Therefore, receiving a Kingdom that can't be shaken, let us have grace, through which we serve God acceptably, with reverence and awe, for our God is a consuming fire.

The Jews were leaving behind the old covenant system that was shaken (removed) to enter the New Covenant system that could not be shaken. At that time, the city of Jerusalem was shaken and burnt by a consuming fire through the Roman armies. At that time the entire Law of Moses passed away, including the ceremonial laws and the Ten Commandments. The "New heaven and earth" was revealed in the New Covenant when the elements of the Temple were melted in the fire.

2nd Peter 3:12-13 "the day of God, which will cause the burning heavens to be dissolved, and the elements will melt with fervent heat? But, according to his promise, we look for new heavens and a new earth, in which righteousness dwells."

The "elements" were all the components of the Law (Temple, sacrifices, priesthood, commandments, Sabbaths, feasts, holy days, seasons, foods) that were described in Galatians 4:3 and Colossians 2:8,16,20. We see how Paul how calls the city of Jerusalem as the old covenant.

*Galatians 4:24-26 "for these are **two covenants. One is from Mount Sinai**, bearing children to bondage, which is Hagar. For this Hagar is Mount Sinai in Arabia, and answers to **the Jerusalem that exists now**, for she is in bondage with her children. But **the Jerusalem that is above is free**, which is the mother of us all."*

The Old heaven and earth was the physical Jerusalem under the Old Covenant. **We live today in Revelation 21:22, in the new heaven and earth that is the New Jerusalem under the New Covenant,** where there is no more Temple or sacrifice in Israel because Christ lives in all of us – we are His body and Temple. **God's righteousness dwells on this earth, because we are righteous in Christ.**

From the wilderness into the Promised Land

It is very common for many believers to think that our life on earth is the wilderness journey before we reach the promised land of salvation. That is because we try to force ourselves into the time of the 1st Century believers who were waiting for the New Covenant to be revealed. The truth is that we are not the Jews who were born under the Law of Moses. When we read the Bible in context, by understanding the transition of Covenants that ended in 70AD, then we will be set free from unnecessary religious burdens. We can find the remarkable parallels between the wilderness journey of Israel in the Old Covenant compared to the journey of the Church in the New Covenant.

1st Corinthians 10:1-5,11 *"Now I would not have you ignorant, brothers, that* ***our fathers were all under the cloud****, and all passed through the sea; and were all baptized into* ***Moses*** *in the cloud and in the sea; and all ate the same spiritual food; and all drank the same spiritual drink. For they drank of a spiritual rock that followed them, and the rock was Christ. However with most of them, God was not well pleased, for they were overthrown in the wilderness.... Now all these things happened to them by way of example, and* ***they were written for our admonition, on whom the ends of the ages have come.****"*

In this scripture, Paul was writing to the Corinthian Jews whose ancestors were led out of Egypt by Moses into the wilderness. We will see the parallels between the Old and New Covenant people in the seven events below:

1) Silence: The Israelites were slaves in Egypt for 430 years. We see that God was silent for those 430 years until He finally sent Moses. There were also 430 years from the time of Malachi until John the Baptist. During that time God did not speak to Israel through any prophets. In Revelation 11, God compares Israel to Egypt in the time of Christ. The people of Israel were slaves under the Law, just like their ancestors were in Egypt.

2) Calling out: Just like Moses called the Hebrews out of Egypt, we see that Christ also called the Church out of Israel. The word "Church" means those who were "called out". They were Jews who were called out of the fading Old Covenant of Israel into the everlasting New Covenant of Christ.

3) Passover: The Israelites received their deliverance from slavery by the blood of the Passover lamb. In the same way, the Church was set free from the slavery of the Law by the blood of the lamb, Jesus Christ. His death on the cross was the true fulfillment of the Passover.

4) Baptism: The Israelites were baptized into Moses by following him through the red sea. In the same way, the Church was baptized into Christ's death and resurrection.

5) Pentecost: Exactly fifty days after Passover, the Israelites received the Ten Commandments (Law of Moses) and 3000 people perished. Exactly fifty days after the cross, the Jewish Church received the Holy Spirit, and 3000 people were saved.

6) Wilderness (trial of faith): The Israelites were in the wilderness for 40 years, fighting against their enemies. The Church was overcoming their enemies (Pharisees) for 40 years in the spiritual wilderness from the cross until 70AD.

7) Promised Land: Joshua led them into the promised land of Canaan, 40 years after leaving Egypt. In the same way, the real "Joshua" came to bring eternal salvation 40 years after the cross. This is because the name "Jesus" is originally known as "Yeshua" or "Joshua", that means "God saves".

*Jeremiah 32:40 NIV "I will make an **everlasting** covenant with them: I will never stop doing good to them"*

The Old Covenant was temporary, and it vanished away after 1500 years. But the New Covenant is an everlasting covenant where God never stops doing good to the human race from generation to generation. Today you are not in the wilderness, but you are already in the promised land; because you are sinless and righteous in Christ.

New Covenant – God alone did the work

*Hebrews 8:6-10,12 "he is also the mediator of a **better covenant**, which on **better promises** has been given as law. For if that first covenant had been faultless, then no place would have been sought for a second. For finding **fault** with them, he said, "Behold, the days come", says the Lord, "that **I will make a new covenant** with the house of Israel and with the house of Judah; **not according to the covenant*** *that I made with their fathers, in the day that I took them by the hand to lead them out of the land of Egypt; **for they didn't continue in my covenant**, and I disregarded them," says the Lord. "For this is the covenant that I will make with the house of Israel…"**I will put my laws into their mind**, I will also write them on their heart … For I will be **merciful** to their unrighteousness. **I will remember their sins and lawless deeds no more."***

Under the Old Covenant, man was at fault because he could not obey the commandments. Therefore God made a New Covenant where He would do everything. In this Covenant, there are no commandments to disobey and therefore no sins to commit! God Himself writes His law of love in the heart. Now we think that God commands us to "love others". But the problem is that if we think of love as a "commandment", then it is not love anymore but an enforced obligation of the law. Love cannot be forced, but it comes by the instinct of our heart. Does a parent need to be told to love his kids? Do lovers need to be told to follow commandments instead of following their hearts? If we think about it, God never told Adam to love Eve but instead told him to stay away from rules and commandments! God told Adam to stay away from religion completely. When Jesus gave the "new commandment", to love one another as He loved them, it was given to the Jews who were under the old covenant. He was showing them that His loving sacrifice was the true fulfillment of the Law. It is His love that manifests effortlessly within us in the New Covenant. I have seen many people display love, even if they have not gone to Church or studied the Bible because God lives in their hearts.

New Covenant – No more separation

The Old Covenant was all about separation because there were "holy" and "unholy" things. Israel was chosen as a holy nation separate from the Gentiles "sinners". But in Christ, a new creation has been formed where there is no Jew or Gentile, but a new humanity where all are righteous. There are no more divisions. All races are perfect and equal in Christ. There are no more religions, but all are one in Christ. There is no difference between male and female in Christ. In the Old Covenant, women were under the authority of their husbands. Today women are leading nations, churches and corporations. In the Law, among all the tribes of the Jews, there was only one priestly tribe who mediated between God and the rest of the people. But in the New Covenant, all of us know God equally well. You are not restricted to God only through pastors, priests, teachers, evangelists or prophets, etc. Your Father lives in you and communicates with you directly. The Father loves all people equally because there is no more sin or judgment or separation between man and God.

Revelation 21:3 "Behold, God's dwelling is with people, and he will dwell with them, and they will be his people, and God himself will be with them as their God"

In the Old Covenant, man was separated from God due to the sins he committed under the Law. The Jews had to offer animal sacrifices that could never take away sins, in a Temple made of stone through an imperfect priest. But then Christ came as the perfect sacrifice and sinless priest who took away all sin. He was the true Temple of God because the Father was one with Christ.

John 2:19-21 "Jesus answered them, "Destroy this temple, and in three days I will raise it up." The Jews therefore said, "It took forty-six years to build this temple! Will you raise it up in three days?" But he spoke of the temple of his body"

After Jesus had risen from the dead, the believers became the body of Christ and Temple of God through the Spirit living in them (1st Corinthians 12:13,27). In 70AD, the Father and Son joined us all to live with us. Now that Christ has taken away sin, God's presence is no longer in the earthly city of Jerusalem and its temple, but He dwells in us. We are the new and spiritual Jerusalem. There is no separation between the Father and us.

New Covenant (Spirit) vs. Old Covenant (Flesh)

I used to be like many Christians who think that we are always fighting this battle between the "flesh" and the "spirit". We think we have a "sinful" nature living along with the new man inside us. But this was only true for the Church who was transitioning between covenants. The reason is that being in the "flesh" was to be under the Law.

Romans 7:1,5 "don't you know, brothers (for I speak to men who know the law) … For when we were in the flesh, the sinful passions which were through the law"

To crucify the flesh, was to trust in Christ by dying to the Law and not trusting in it anymore.

Galatians 2:19-20 "For I, through the law, died to the law, that I might live to God. I have been crucified with Christ, and it is no longer I that live, but Christ living in me"

The believers were called out of the Law by faith in Christ to enter the New Covenant, and they were in the "Spirit" because their flesh was put away on the cross.

Romans 8:9 "you are not in the flesh but in the Spirit"

Colossians 2:13 "You were dead through your trespasses and the uncircumcision of your flesh. He made you alive together with him, having forgiven us all our trespasses"

But before 70AD, they could go back to the flesh by going back under the Law due to the persecution from the Pharisees. This was the battle between the flesh and the Spirit for the believers. In 70AD, the Law, sin and the flesh finally passed away when God made the New Covenant.

*Isaiah 59:21 NIV ""As for me, this is my **covenant** with them," says the LORD. "**My Spirit, who is on you, will not depart from you**, and my words that I have put in your mouth will always be on your lips, on the lips of your children and on the lips of their descendants — from this time on and forever," says the LORD."*

Today all of us are in the Spirit of Grace in the New Covenant. We cannot go back to the flesh anymore because we are in the Spirit permanently where God lives in us forever throughout all the generations that live in this world. The Spirit of Christ has defeated the flesh of the Law.

New Covenant – No more sin!

Christ died for the people who sinned under the Old Covenant (Hebrews 9:7). In 70AD, the New Covenant was established, and God no longer accounts sin to Israel or the human race.

*Hebrews 10:16-17 ""**This is the covenant** that I will make with them: 'After those days,' says the Lord, 'I will put my laws on their heart, I will also write them on their mind;'" then he says, "**I will remember their sins and their iniquities no more.**"*

We were not born under the Law that accounts sin because the Old Covenant does not exist anymore. Every human being since 70AD has been born in the New Covenant. We were not enemies of God under the Old Covenant. We did not crucify Christ, but it was the people under the Law who crucified Him. He died for the people who committed sins under the Law.

Romans 4:15 "because the law brings wrath. And where there is no law there is no transgression."

Sin was the breaking of the Law (1st John 3:4). This Law and its wrath ended in 70AD, and therefore there is no more transgression of the Law.

Sin does not exist anymore! Now, of course, this does not mean that people are perfect in behavior. We may do stupid things to hurt one another or ourselves, but we cannot sin against God because the Law does not exist. Someone told me that this made him free to kill and steal. I reminded him that the government authorities protect society from criminals. If the Ten Commandments were needed today and if it could save humanity, then Christ need not have come to the earth. But Christ came because the Law could never make anyone holy (Hebrews 7:19). The Jews, who had the Law, were the ones who rejected God's love but the lawless pagan Gentiles were the ones who believed.

2nd Corinthians 5:17-19,21 ***"Therefore if anyone is in Christ, he is a new creation. The old things have passed away. Behold, all things have become new.*** *But all things are of God, who reconciled us to himself through Jesus Christ, and gave to us the ministry of reconciliation; namely, that* ***God was in Christ reconciling the world to himself, not reckoning to them their trespasses … For him who knew no sin he made to be sin on our behalf; so that in him we might become the righteousness of God."***

The Law imputed sins, but the Love of God in Christ took away the sins of the world. His love keeps no record of sins and that is why His love was the fulfillment of the Law. That is why the Law is finished. His love offered the sacrifice to satisfy the Law and make a New Covenant where there is no more Law and therefore no more sin. God has made a New Covenant where if anyone is in Christ, then they are new creations without any more sin. Now you may say that not everyone is in Christ.

Romans 5:18 "So then as through one trespass, ALL men were condemned; even so through one act of righteousness, ***ALL men were justified to life"***

All humanity was born in "sin" because they were in Adam. They committed "sins" by specific transgressions of the Law of Moses (Ten Commandments). But Christ was the last Adam who took away the "sin" of Adam. He also took away the "sins" under the Law by fulfilling the Law. Jesus died on the Cross and destroyed the Old Covenant in 70AD, thereby removing the old order and making all things new. Now under the New Covenant, ALL of humanity was made righteous by Christ's one act of obedience. There is no more tree of knowledge of good and evil. Jesus has restored the tree of life to all of humanity. **We were not even born in Adam. We were not born in sin. We were all born in Christ.** We were born in Christ's righteousness without any sin. There was never a time in your life when you were in sin. You have been perfect in Christ all the time!

Let me explain this in a different way. As a Computer Science student, one of the first things we were taught was the binary number system. In this system, there are only two numbers: 0 and 1. The number 0 means nothing and the number 1 means everything. There is no in-between and no shades of gray. You're either in or out. In the Old Creation and Old Covenant, all men were guilty as "zeroes". But now in the New Creation and New Covenant, there are no sinners because Christ is the "One" who made us all righteous by His obedience.

Jesus has removed sin by making a New Covenant

Chapter 3

End times are over

I still remember that night. After my long prayer, I would ask the Lord to speak to me directly through the Bible. I opened the pages, and it said that Jesus was coming soon. This happened for many days repeatedly, so I was sure that God was telling me that the "End" was near. I had to warn all my friends and Church members about the second coming of Christ. I started sending emails and making YouTube videos warning them to stop sinning and be ready for the Lord who was coming soon!

The Last Days were 2000 years ago.

In the last 40 years, we have had several end-of-the-world predictions. People have left their jobs and sold their possessions, only to be proven wrong. Every generation for the last 2000 years has said that "Jesus is coming" because they thought they were living in the last days. But what about the people like John, Peter & Paul, who all prophesied that Jesus was coming soon in their lifetime? Were they unreliable? Why would an atheist want to believe us when Christianity has been wrong for 2000 years? We have become a laughing stock because we keep saying that Jesus is coming back every year and nothing happens. Let's see what the Bible talks about the last days.

*Hebrews 1:1-2 NIV "In the past God spoke to our ancestors through the prophets at many times and in various ways, but in **these last days** he has spoken to us by his Son"*

God spoke to the Hebrews through the Old Covenant Law and the prophets for 1500 years, but in "these" last days, He spoke to them through Christ. So it is clear that the "last days" were 2000 years ago. The last days were the end times of the Old Covenant. The Law of Moses lasted for 1500 years and therefore the last days could not span another 2000 years. What did Jesus preach to the Jews? It was about a New Covenant where God would take away their sins.

The Bible is full of evidence that those people were living in the last days. Peter and James were apostles who wrote specifically to the Jews, and they proclaimed that they were living in the last days and that the end was near.

1st Peter 4:7 "But the end of all things is near."
James 5:3 "You have laid up your treasure in the last days."

But the modern teaching is that these "last days" began on the cross and have continued for 2000 years because "1 day" in God's eyes is a "thousand years" on earth, and hence 2000 years translate to 2 days in God's plan. Well, there's a big problem with that logic. John actually said that they were in the last hour!

*1st John 2:18-19, 22 NASB "Children, **IT IS the last hour**; and just as you heard that antichrist is coming, even **now** many antichrists have appeared; **from this we know that it is the last hour**. They went out from us, but they were not really of us... Who is the liar but the one who denies that Jesus is the Christ? This is the antichrist, the one who denies the Father and the Son."*

John clearly wrote that it was the "last hour" before the "end". His proof was that the "antichrists" were appearing all over the place. Well, who was this antichrist? Was it one of the US Presidents or the Pope or some suave European leader bringing peace to the Middle East? No, it was someone who was known to the people of the 1st century. In fact, John made it very clear that it was the Jews who left the Church to return to the Old Covenant. The definition of "antichrist" was the one who denied that Christ was the Messiah of Israel. It was referring to the Pharisees and many Jews who crucified Him and persecuted the Church. These Jews rejected the words of Christ and the apostles who warned Israel that they were living in the last days! In fact, Peter talked about these scoffers who were the unbelieving Jews who mocked the 2nd coming of Christ.

2nd Peter 3:3-4,8-9 NLT "Most importantly, I want to remind you that in the last days scoffers will come, mocking the truth and following their own desires. They will say, "What happened to the promise that Jesus is coming again? From before *the times of **our ancestors**, everything has remained the same since the world was first created ... But you must not forget this one thing, dear friends: A day is like a thousand years to the Lord, and a thousand years is like a day. The Lord isn't really being slow about his promise, as some people think. No, he is being patient for **your sake**. He does not want anyone to be destroyed, but wants everyone to repent."*

The promise of "1 day" being a "1000 years" was written to the Jews and not to us. When Jesus came, the Jews were under the Law for more than 1000 years, and the end was near for them. The judgment and resurrection of the Old Covenant were imminent. These Jewish scoffers looked back at the history of their fathers from the time of Moses and said that everything would continue as before and that their nation would still be God's chosen people. They did not expect the old covenant to end. But God told the Jews, that they were living in the last days. It was their last chance to be saved because of His great mercy. They were called to repent because Christ's coming was near.

Their Generation, not ours

Now, whenever a rapture prediction fails, we will point to Christ's declaration that no one can know the day or the hour. But, Christ made two statements that will clarify the truth.

John 16:12-13 "I have yet many things to tell you, but you can't bear them now. However when he, the Spirit of truth, has come, he will guide you into all truth"

Jesus told the apostles that although He could not reveal the exact day and hour, the Holy Spirit would tell them all things. And we see that in the Epistles, where John was telling the Jews that they were living in the last hour. Paul also wrote to the Thessalonians and Corinthians that they would personally be alive until the coming of the Lord.

*1st Corinthians 1:7-8 "so that **you** come behind in no gift; **waiting** for the revelation of our Lord Jesus Christ; who will also confirm you until the end, blameless in the day of our Lord Jesus Christ."*

*1st Thessalonians 5:23-24 "May **your** whole spirit, soul, and body be preserved blameless at the **coming** of our Lord Jesus Christ. He who calls **you** is faithful, who will also do it."*

In fact, Paul also told the Romans that they were living in that time just before Christ's 2nd coming.

*Romans 13:11-12 NASB "Do this, knowing the time, that **it is already the hour** for you to awaken from sleep; for **now** salvation is nearer to us than when we believed. The night is almost gone and the day is **near**"*

The Romans had believed the Gospel a certain number of years before Paul's letter to them. Now, Paul was telling them that they were living in the hour before they received the salvation! It was closer than the time since they believed. This clearly proves that the last day and hour was within their generation. Jesus also promised that their generation would be the one to fulfill it.

*Matthew 24:34-36 "Most certainly I tell you, **this generation will not pass away, until all these things are accomplished**. Heaven and earth will pass away, but my words will not pass away. But no one knows of that day and hour... but my Father only."*

Jesus emphatically said that "this generation" to whom He was speaking, would see all things happen. He was not talking about our generation. We know that the passing away of the "heaven and earth" was a reference to the destruction of the Old Covenant system. When we read the Bible in context by looking at the previous chapter, we see the clearest proof that He was talking about their time and not 2016.

*Matthew 23:29, 35-38 "Woe to you, **scribes and Pharisees**, hypocrites ... I send to you prophets, wise men, and scribes. Some of them **you will kill and crucify**; and some of them you will scourge in your synagogues, and persecute from city to city; **that on you may come all the righteous blood shed on the earth**, from the blood of righteous Abel to the blood of Zachariah son of Barachiah, whom you killed between the sanctuary and the altar. **Most certainly I tell you, all these things will come upon this generation.** "**Jerusalem, Jerusalem,** who kills the prophets, and stones those who are sent to her! How often I would have gathered your children together, even as a hen gathers her chicks under her wings, and you would not! **Behold, your house is left to you desolate.**"*

Jesus clearly said that the generation of the Pharisees would be held responsible for all the persecution of God's people from the time of Abel till Christ's death on the cross and the persecution of the Church. The judgment would fall upon that generation through the destruction of the Temple in 70AD. Now some will say that this generation means the "Jewish race" and that the people of Israel in 2016 are also going to be judged. First of all, the Bible defines a "generation" as a 40-year period. In Matthew 1, the genealogy of David until Christ shows 28 generations spanning approximately 1000 years. This results in roughly 40 years per generation. Guess how many years were between Christ's preaching and 70AD? 40 years or exactly one generation! This is why Peter and Paul called that generation a wicked and corrupt generation (Acts 2:40, Philippians 2:15). It was talking about the Pharisees and not us today.

Those who pierced Christ saw His 2nd coming

*John 19:36-37 "For these things happened, that the Scripture might be fulfilled, "A bone of him will not be broken." Again another Scripture says, "They will look on him whom **they pierced**."*

The Jewish people of today have nothing to do with the crucifixion of Christ. The Pharisees and the High Priests crucified Jesus almost 2000 years ago. To say that God will judge the Jews of 2016 is a matter of terrible injustice. Would it make any sense to condemn the people of Germany today for Hitler's crimes in the 1930s? Would it be fair to punish the Italians today for the atrocities committed 2000 years ago, by the Roman Empire? This is why Jesus said that it would be their specific generation that would witness His 2nd coming.

Revelation 1:7 "Behold, he is coming with the clouds, and every eye will see him, including those who pierced him. All the tribes of the earth (land) will mourn over him. Even so, Amen."

The Jews who pierced Christ were the same people who witnessed His 2nd coming. Now does that mean that it was a global event where everyone in the world saw Him? If so, why was it not recorded in world history? It's because His coming was only seen by those who pierced Him in the land of Israel. The tribes refer to the 12 tribes of Israel.

*Zechariah 12:10-14 NASB "I will pour out on the house of David and on **the inhabitants of Jerusalem**, the Spirit of grace and of supplication, so that **they will look on Me whom they have pierced; and they will mourn** for Him, as one mourns for an only son, and they will weep bitterly over Him like the bitter weeping over a firstborn. **In that day there will be great mourning in Jerusalem**, like the mourning of Hadadrimmon in the plain of Megiddo. **The land will mourn, every family (tribe) by itself**; the family of the house of David by itself and their wives by themselves; the family of the house of Nathan by itself and their wives by themselves; the family of the house of Levi by itself and their wives by themselves; the family of the Shimeites by itself and their wives by themselves; all the families that remain, **every family (tribe)** by itself and their wives by themselves."*

The mourning happened in Jerusalem, and it happened in every family or tribe of Israel in the land. It was not talking about the entire world, but only in Israel. Peter confirmed this when he preached on the Day of Pentecost to all the Jews in Jerusalem who had crucified Jesus. He warned that specific generation to believe in Christ to be saved from the judgment of 70AD.

*Acts 2:36,40 "Let all the house of **Israel** therefore know certainly that God has made him both Lord and Christ, this Jesus whom **you crucified**. ... With many other words he testified, and exhorted them, saying, "Save yourselves from **this** crooked generation!"*

Christ also spoke similar words to that generation of Jews. They were the only people who witnessed Christ and the Apostles, and yet they crucified and persecuted them. They were constantly asking for signs but remained in unbelief. Jesus promised that His 2nd coming would happen to the same generation who rejected His 1st coming – the Pharisees.

*Mark 8:11-12, 38 "**The Pharisees** came out and began to question him, seeking from him a sign from heaven, and testing him. He sighed deeply in his spirit, and said, "Why does **this generation** seek a sign? Most certainly I tell you, **no sign will be given to this generation** ... For whoever will be ashamed of me and of my words in **this adulterous and sinful generation**, the Son of Man also will be ashamed of him, **when he comes** in his Father's glory, with the holy angels."*

You see; there is nothing for you to be afraid. Even if you may not have testified about Christ or were afraid to do so, it was that specific generation who were judged in His 2nd coming.

Christ's 2nd coming at the Destruction of the Temple

The passage of Matthew 24 is one of the most famous and yet misunderstood passages in the entire Bible. Movies have been made, and books have been sold based on this passage about the 2nd coming of Christ. Whenever an earthquake happens, we are told that the "End" is near, based on Matthew 24. In that chapter, Christ warned His disciples that the sign of His coming would be wars, earthquakes, famines, false Messiahs, and persecution. What is unknown to many Christians is that the historical records of Josephus show that all these things happened in the Roman Empire in that generation. In the Book of Acts, there was a great famine (Acts 11:28). The history of the Jews tells us that they had several rebellious wars against the Roman occupiers before their destruction in 70AD (Matthew 27:38, Mark 15:7, Luke 13:1, Acts 21:38). Many false messiahs tried to deceive the Jews during that time. Paul wrote to the Thessalonians that the 2nd coming of Christ would happen immediately after the false Messiah sat in the Temple that existed in Jerusalem at the time when he wrote this epistle.

2nd *Thessalonians 2:1-4,8 NASB "Now we request you, brethren, with regard to* **the coming of our Lord Jesus Christ** *and our gathering together to Him, that you not be quickly shaken from your composure or be disturbed either by a spirit or a message or a letter as if from us, to the effect that the day of the Lord has come. Let no one in any way deceive you,* **for it will not come unless the apostasy comes first**, *and the* **man of lawlessness is revealed**, *the son of destruction, who opposes and exalts himself above every so-called god or object of worship, so that* **he takes his seat in the temple of God**, *displaying himself as being God ... Then that lawless one will be revealed whom the Lord will slay with the breath of His mouth and bring to an end by the appearance of His coming;"*

Jesus had predicted that there would be a great falling away of the Jews from the faith. In 2nd Timothy 3, Paul described the last days in their time when the people of God would be lovers of money and law-breakers. This was the perfect description of the Pharisees (Luke 16:14, Matthew 15:16) who fell away and worshiped the "false Messiah" who sat in the Temple in Jerusalem. This was most probably the Jew named "John Levi of Gischala" who was responsible for the rebellion of the Jews that resulted in the destruction of the Temple by the Romans. He tried to be the Messiah of the Jews in fighting a battle against the Romans so that he could set up the kingdom in Jerusalem. This happened exactly as Christ and Paul predicted.

In Matthew 24:3, the question posed by the disciples was a three-fold question: *"Tell us, when will these things be? What is the sign of your coming, and of the end of the age?"*

Many scholars view it as three separate events, but the Bible confirms that they were all about the same incident – the destruction of the Temple in Jerusalem in 70AD. This was the 2nd coming of Christ at the end of the "age" of the Old Covenant. It was not the end of the world but the last day of the Law.

Mark 13:1-4 *"***As he went out of the temple***, one of his disciples said to him, "Teacher, see what kind of stones and what kind of buildings!" Jesus said to him, "Do you see these great buildings?* **There will not be left here one stone on another, which will not be thrown down.***" As he sat on the Mount of Olives opposite the temple, Peter, James, John, and Andrew asked him privately,* **"Tell us, when will these things be? What is the sign that these things are ALL about to be fulfilled?"**

That was the event when all things in the Bible would be fulfilled. As Christ Himself testified here:

*Luke 21:20,22 "But **when you see Jerusalem surrounded by armies**, then know that its desolation is at hand ... **ALL** things which are written may be **fulfilled**."*

The 2nd coming of Christ was the destruction of the Temple by the Roman armies in 70AD.

*Revelation 11:2,3,18 "Leave out the court which is outside of the **temple**, and don't measure it ... They will tread the holy **city** under foot for forty-two months ... where also their Lord was **crucified** ... The nations were angry, and your wrath came, as did the time for the dead to be judged"*

When the Jewish rulers and false Messiah trampled the Temple of Jerusalem for 42 months before 70AD and killed the witnesses of Christ, it was the time when the wrath of God came upon them, and the dead were raised in the final judgment.

*Isaiah 66:6,15,22 NIV "Hear that uproar from the city, hear that **noise from the temple**! It is the sound of the L*ORD* repaying his enemies all they deserve ... See, the L*ORD* is coming with fire, and his **chariots** are like a whirlwind; ... **the new heavens and the new earth** that I make will endure before me"*

The new covenant (heaven and earth) was created when the Temple was destroyed in the 2nd coming of Christ. That was the Day of the Lord when the old covenant passed away.

*Matthew 24:33 NASB "so, you too, when you **see** all these things, recognize that **He is near, right at the door.**"*

Christ said that when they would see those things occurring in and around Jerusalem, they would know that His coming was imminent and right at the door! When James wrote to the 12 tribes of Israel, he told them that the moment had finally come!

*James 5:8-9 "You also be patient. Establish your hearts, **for the coming of the Lord is at hand**. Don't grumble, brothers, against one another, so that you won't be judged. Behold, **the judge stands at the door**."*

This was confirmed in the Book of Revelation where Christ told two Churches in Asia, that He was standing at the door just before His 2nd

coming. It happened in their lifetime because those Churches do not exist anymore.

*Revelation 3:10-12, 20 "Because you kept my command to endure, I also will keep you from the hour of testing, which is to come on the whole world, to test those who dwell on the earth. **I am coming quickly!** Hold firmly that which you have, so that no one takes your crown. …. **Behold, I stand at the door and knock"***

Christ's 2nd coming was promised only to those who saw Him ascend into heaven.

*Acts 1:11 "You men of Galilee, why do you stand looking into the sky? This Jesus, who was received up from you into the sky will come back in the same way **as you saw** him going into the sky."*

He returned to those same people in the clouds in 70AD. **He did not return in flesh and blood but in the Spirit**. When Jesus was raised from the dead, it was in the same body of flesh and bone (Luke 24:39). This happened as a sign to the Jews to prove to them that Jesus was the Messiah. Just like Jonah was inside the whale for three days and came back in the same body, Jesus also was raised back in the same body three days after His death (Matthew 12:40). But when Jesus ascended to heaven, He returned to the heavenly glory that He had always possessed. This was proven when Paul met Christ on the road to Damascus and saw a glorious light instead of a man with flesh and bones. John also saw Christ in his heavenly glory in the Spirit in Revelation 1:12-16. This description matches the heavenly glory of God that was seen in Ezekiel 1:25-29. The truth is that God is Spirit and He made a New Covenant where we became His spiritual temple so that He lives with all of us at the same time. If Jesus came back physically and sat in a physical temple, then it would be impossible for Him to be with billions of people at the same time. Therefore His return in 70AD had to be spiritual, and this manifested in the destruction of the Temple.

The faithful promise of Christ

Imagine if I promised my children that I would go away on a business trip and come back to them one day. Now imagine if I did not keep my promise for 2000 years. Guess what I would be called? An unfaithful, unreliable father who did not keep his promises! The truth is that Jesus promised His disciples that He would come back for them. These were the disciples with whom He had spent three years teaching about the kingdom of God. He loved them and gave His life for them, and finally, He made a promise to return to them. If Jesus did not keep His promise to those with whom

He lived with, then how can we say that He was faithful? The 1st Century Church were the ones who deserved it more than anyone else. They were suffering all over the world by dying for Christ at the hands of the Jews and Romans. If there was one generation who desperately needed His coming, it was the 1st Century Church. He promised it only to them as the Bible clearly states here:

Matthew 10:5,23 *"Jesus sent **these twelve** out…to the lost sheep of Israel … when they persecute you in this city, flee into the next, for most certainly I tell you, **you will not have gone through the cities of Israel, until the Son of Man has come.**"*

The Jewish disciples were sent to preach to their fellow Jews and were promised great persecution from city to city. Christ promised them that His coming would happen before they finished preaching in Israel. They were not able to finish preaching in Israel before 70AD when they had to flee the coming destruction of the Roman armies.

Matthew 16:28 *"Most certainly I tell you, there are some standing here who will in no way taste of death, until they see the Son of Man coming in his Kingdom."*

Jesus emphatically told those 12 disciples that some of them would remain alive till He came back. None of them are alive today unless they are 2000 years old, which is impossible. We know that most of the disciples like Peter, James and even Paul passed away before 70AD. From John 21:21-24, it is clear that John would only die after he saw the 2nd coming of Christ. The Bible proves that John died after this event.

Matthew 26:62,64 *"The High Priest stood up …. Jesus said to him, "You have said it. Nevertheless, I tell you, after this you will see the Son of Man sitting at the right hand of Power, and coming on the clouds of the sky."*

Jesus clearly told the High Priest of Israel that he would personally see Him coming in the clouds. During the great tribulation of 70AD, the Jews cried out for their Messiah saying *"Blessed is He who comes in the name of the Lord"* (Matthew 23:39). That is when they saw Christ coming in the clouds, and they mourned bitterly because they finally realized that Jesus was the Lord and Messiah.

So then, the questions remain. Was Jesus faithful? Can God's words be trusted? The Bible has been accurate when it prophesied the events of Christ's 1st coming. When Jesus was born to a virgin, it was the fulfillment of prophecy. His healing, miracles, betrayal by Judas, death on the cross and resurrection were also predicted before it happened. Every Christian believes that Jesus was faithful in fulfilling God's word in His birth, death and resurrection. But when it comes to Christ's 2nd coming, we have dragged it on for 2000 years, putting His name and faithfulness in question.

*Revelation 22:20 "He who **testifies** these things says, "Yes, I come **quickly**."*

The Bible is very clear – Jesus testified to the 1st Century Church that He would come quickly. He did not lie or exaggerate. The truth is that He was faithful in His 2nd coming in 70AD.

End of Israel, and not the world

When we study Matthew 24, we can often interpret it as a "universe ending" catastrophe because we read things like the darkening of the sun & moon, the falling of stars to the earth and the shaking of the heavens. But we have to realize that the Bible was written by the Jews using the language of the Old Testament and not modern Christian theology or the English language. This is what was prophesied in the Old Testament when the Roman armies would attack Jerusalem in 70AD:

*Joel 2:1-2,7,9-11 NASB "For the **day of the** LORD is coming; Surely it is near, A day of darkness and gloom, A day of clouds and thick darkness. So there is a great and mighty people ... They climb the wall like **soldiers** ... They rush on the **city** ... Before them the earth quakes, The heavens tremble, The sun and the moon grow dark And the stars lose their brightness. The LORD utters His voice before His **army**;"*

The day of the Lord was described as a day when the Lord's army would attack the city of Jerusalem, and the sun, moon and stars would grow dark. Peter also quoted the prophet Joel in Acts 2 on the Day of Pentecost when the Holy Spirit was given to Israel in Jerusalem.

Acts 2:16-17, 20 "But THIS is what has been spoken through the prophet Joel: 'It will be in the last days, says God that I will pour out my spirit on all flesh.... The sun will be turned into darkness, and the moon into blood, before the great and glorious day of the Lord comes."

He told those Jews who were living in Jerusalem during those last days, to call upon the name of the Lord to be saved because the same events in Matthew 24 and Joel 2 were about to happen in their generation. Now, what was the meaning of the term "sun, moon and stars"? It was symbolically referring to Israel, as Joseph explained to his brothers in the Old Testament.

*Genesis 37:9-10 "Behold, I have dreamed yet another dream: and behold, the **sun and the moon and eleven stars** bowed down to me. He told it to his father and to his brothers. His father rebuked him, and said to him, "What is this dream that you have dreamed? Will **I and your mother and your brothers** indeed come to bow ourselves down to you to the earth?"*

According to the Bible, the "sun, moon and stars" referred to Jacob and his sons. It was Jacob who was named Israel, and he had 12 sons who represented each tribe of Israel. The darkening of the sun, moon and stars was referring to the destruction of the nation of Israel under the Old Covenant.

We can also see an amazing similarity in Isaiah 13, where it talks about the destruction of Babylon by the Persians, hundreds of years before Christ was born.

*Isaiah 13:1,4,10,17 NIV "A prophecy against Babylon ... The Lord Almighty is mustering an **army** for war ... See the day of the Lord is coming ... The stars of heaven and their constellations will not show their light. The rising **sun will be darkened** and the moon will not give its light ... See I will stir up against them, the Medes (**Persians**)"*

The destruction of the Babylonian kingdom by the Persians was described by highly symbolic and apocalyptic language. It talks of the sun and the moon being darkened as a symbolic description of the destruction of Babylon by the Persians.

Isaiah 34:4,9 NIV "All the stars in the sky will be dissolved and the heavens rolled up like a scroll; all the starry host will fall ... Edom's streams will be turned into pitch"

When foreign armies destroyed the nation of Edom, Isaiah described it like the stars falling to earth and the heavens being rolled up like a scroll of paper. Of course, we know that nothing like this could have happened because the earth still exists today. Could a star that is million times larger than the earth fall on us? No, of course not. This is the symbolic language of the destruction of a kingdom and not the end of the world.

In Revelation 6, there is an amazing parallel compared to the events of Matthew 24. There are false Messiahs, famines, violence, earthquakes and persecution that are described almost identically in the two chapters, proving that they are both talking about the same event of 70AD. This chapter ends with Christ's 2nd coming described as falling mountains on the earth.

Revelation 6:16 "They told the mountains and the rocks, "Fall on us, and hide us from the face of him who sits on the throne, and from the wrath of the Lamb"

We read this and think that mountains are going to fall on the face of the entire earth. But we see how Jesus was talking about the destruction of Jerusalem in 70AD and not the whole earth.

*Luke 23:28-30 "Jesus, turning to them, said, **"Daughters of Jerusalem**, don't weep for me, but **weep for yourselves** and for your children. For behold, **the days are coming** in which they will say, 'Blessed are the barren, the wombs that never bore, and the breasts that never nursed.' **Then they will begin to tell the mountains, 'Fall on us!'** and tell the hills, 'Cover us.'*

The "falling mountains" were the apocalyptic language where the Jews pronounced judgment on themselves. It was not about a literal mountain that fell on them.

Some of us say that Christ's 2nd coming should have been visible to all the nations and not just Israel, like the lightning flashes from east to west as written in Matthew 24. But the historian Josephus clearly recorded great signs in the skies over Jerusalem in 70AD, including the presence of Angelic armies and chariots. There were no such signs anywhere else. The Bible also tells us what exactly was the "sign" of "lightning".

Ezekiel 21:28 NASB "Thus says the Lord GOD concerning the sons of Ammon and concerning their reproach,' and say: 'A sword, a sword is drawn, polished for the slaughter, to cause it to consume, that it may be like lightning"

Josephus recorded that a bright sword was hovering over the skies of Jerusalem shining like lightning, telling the Jews that their nation was going to be destroyed by the sword of the Roman armies. At that time, Josephus recorded that the presence of God departed from the Temple in Jerusalem.

The Clouds of God's presence came to be with us

The Lord's coming in the "clouds" had two meanings according to the Old Testament:

Isaiah 30:27,31 NIV "See, the Name of the LORD comes from afar, with burning anger and dense clouds of smoke … the voice of the Lord will shatter Assyria"

The first meaning was that the Lord's presence would come in the form of judgment through foreign armies. The verse above talks about the destruction of the Assyrians before Israel was exiled to Babylon. So when Jesus told the Jews that they would see Him coming in the clouds, they knew that He was pronouncing judgment through a foreign army, which happened in 70AD. The judgment of the Lord through an army was compared to His voice. This is what Paul wrote in 2nd Thessalonians 2:8 when he said that the breath of the Lord through the Roman army would destroy the antichrist (false messiah) who sat in the Jerusalem Temple in 70AD.

1st Kings 8:11 NASB "the priests could not stand to minister because of the cloud, for the glory of the LORD filled the house of the LORD."

The second meaning of "the cloud" was the presence of God in the Temple in Jerusalem. When Jesus talked about the destruction of the Temple and the coming in the clouds, He was telling the Jews that the presence of God was no longer in the Old Covenant Temple. His presence was now in the body of Christ, in the New Jerusalem where God would no longer dwell in buildings but He would live among the people. The 2nd coming of Christ was the transfer of God's presence from the Temple and poured out through His Spirit to all humanity.

John 14:23 "My Father will love him, and we will come to him, and make our home with him"

God does not dwell in Jerusalem anymore, but the Father has made you His dwelling place. You are His "home sweet home".

The Rapture–to be one with Christ

I loved to watch the "Left Behind" movies where the Church was suddenly raptured out of the earth before the great tribulation and destruction of the planet. But when we study Church history, the doctrine of the rapture was introduced in the 1800s. It originated from a girl in Britain who had a dream and was promoted by theologians like Darby and Schofield. The rapture says that God will remove the Christians from the earth and deal with Israel once again and that they will rebuild a third Temple in Jerusalem. But this doctrine is not Biblical. In Matthew 24, it clearly said that the generation of the Apostles would experience the great tribulation in Israel and that the 2nd coming of Christ was immediately after the tribulation in 70AD. There is also no Biblical proof of a third Temple.

John 4:21-24 "Jesus said to her, "Woman, believe me, the hour comes, when neither in this mountain, nor in Jerusalem, will you worship the Father. You worship that which you don't know. We worship that which we know; for salvation is from the Jews. But the hour comes, and now is, when the true worshipers will worship the Father in spirit and truth, for the Father seeks such to be his worshipers. God is spirit, and those who worship him must worship in spirit and truth."

Jesus told the Samaritan woman that God would no longer be worshiped in Jerusalem but that He would dwell with us in Spirit and truth. Paul also said that the New Jerusalem was referring to the New Covenant, but the Old Jerusalem was the Old Covenant (Galatians 4:21-27). God took away the Old Covenant in 70AD by destroying the Temple. He will not be dealing with Israel anymore because we live in the New Covenant where the Temple and sacrifices came to an end.

The word "rapture" does not exist in the Bible. The actual word was to be "caught up" with the Lord or to be in His presence. Both Paul and John were caught up with the Lord in the Spirit, and not physically (2nd Corinthians 12:2-4, Revelation 4:1). They did not leave their physical bodies, but it was to be with the Lord in spirit. Now, during the 40-year wilderness journey of the Church from the cross till 70AD, they were transitioning between Old and New Covenant. God had given them the Holy Spirit as a deposit of the inheritance (Ephesians 1:14). The Holy Spirit was their comforter during the great persecution and tribulation. But they were not yet with united with Christ because they were waiting for His 2nd coming. As long as the Temple stood in Jerusalem, God's presence could not fully be united with men. The only thing separating them from unity with God was the Old Covenant.

The Old Covenant was the ministry of Satan because it was the Law and the Ten Commandments that brought condemnation and accusation to the world (John 5:45, 2nd Corinthians 3:7-9). The Pharisees and High Priests were the "brood of vipers" or the "messengers of Satan" (Matthew 23:23, 2nd Corinthians 11:13-14). The kingdom of Satan was the Old Covenant and its temple where the false Jewish messiah was worshiped before 70AD. Satan was the "prince of the power of the air" in the heavenly places that ruled the world. When Jesus returned in 70AD, He destroyed the Temple and His Spirit came to dwell with all men.

*Ephesians 2:1-6 "You were made alive when you were dead in transgressions and sins, in which you once walked according to the course of this world, according to the **prince of the power of the air**, the spirit who now works in the children of disobedience; among whom we also all once lived in the lust of our flesh, doing the* *desires of the flesh and of the mind, and were by nature children of wrath, even as the rest. But God, being rich in mercy, for his great love with which he loved us, even when we were dead through our trespasses,* **made us alive together with Christ** *(by grace you have been saved), and raised us up with him, and made us* **to sit with him in the heavenly places in Christ Jesus"**

The Church was seated with Christ in heavenly places, and we were all spiritually "caught up" or raptured from the Old Covenant system into the New Covenant. They met Christ in the "air" and replaced Satan as the ruler of the world. Paul wrote to the Romans that "Satan" was going to be crushed under the feet of the Church very soon, in their lifetime.

Romans 16:20 NLT "The God of peace will **soon crush Satan** *under* **your feet***. May the grace of our Lord Jesus be with you"*

This happened during the destruction of the Old Covenant, its temple and the Pharisees. That was when the Grace of our Lord Jesus came to take away the Law in 70AD.

Revelation 22:20-21 "Amen! Yes, come, Lord Jesus. The grace of the Lord Jesus Christ be with all the saints. Amen."

We were caught up in the spirit to become one with Christ in the New Covenant. There is no future rapture because we are already one with Christ in this life and forever.

The Revelation of Jesus Christ's Grace

The Book of Revelation is one of the most difficult and confusing books in the Bible. Many people stay away from Revelation because it causes debates, confusion and fear. There have been many different interpretations by the Church over the last 300 years. But the problem is that we cannot interpret this book by watching CNN, the Middle East or denominational bias. This is because it was not written to us directly and it was not talking about events in the 21st century.

Revelation 1:1-4 NIV "The revelation from Jesus Christ, which God gave him to show his servants **what must soon take place***. He made it known by sending his angel to his servant John, who testifies to* **everything** *he saw – that is, the word of God and the* **testimony** *of Jesus Christ. Blessed is the one who reads aloud the words of this prophecy, and blessed are those who hear it and take to heart what is written in it, because* **the time is near***. John, To the seven churches in the province of Asia:"*

The Book of Revelation was the testimony of Christ who said that everything that was written was supposed to happen soon. It was not written to us, but to the seven churches of Asia. Now some people say that these seven churches are the different Church ages that existed over the last 2000 years. But the truth is that Jesus told John that the "time is near", which clearly indicates that it was about to happen in their lifetime and not across 2000 years of history. Remember that Christ told the Apostles that all things would be fulfilled when the Roman armies surrounded Jerusalem in their generation (Luke 21:22).

Revelation 1:9 NASB " I, John, your brother and fellow partaker in the tribulation"

The Great tribulation is not going to happen in the future. John was already experiencing the tribulation when he wrote Revelation 2000 years ago. We also know that the Thessalonians were in the tribulation because Paul wrote to them that they would personally get relief from the persecution when Jesus was revealed in the blazing fire to destroy their enemies, the Pharisees (2nd Thessalonians 1:7). In fact, Paul told all his Churches that they had to endure the tribulation to enter the kingdom (Acts 14:20-22). Paul also wrote in 1st Thessalonians 2:14-16, that the wrath had finally come upon the Jews who were persecuting the Church all over the Roman Empire. Jesus also told the Jews that the great tribulation of their generation would never be repeated (Matthew 24:21). This comprehensively proves that the events of Revelation were all fulfilled within the 1st Century and will never be repeated.

Although the traditions say that the book of Revelation was written in 95AD, the Bible clearly indicates that it was written before 70AD. In Revelation 11, John talks about the trampling of the Temple for 42 months and the killing of apostles/witnesses in the city where Christ was crucified. This clearly shows that the Temple existed in Jerusalem when John wrote Revelation. History shows us that the city was under attack for exactly 42 months before 70AD. Jerusalem was the city where Jesus was crucified before it was destroyed in 70AD. There was also great persecution of Christians in Jerusalem during that time that was never repeated. **This proves that John wrote this before 70AD**. In fact, all scripture was written before this event. In John 5:2, he wrote about the existence of a pool in Jerusalem, which indicates that he wrote it before 70AD. In 1st John 4:17, he wrote about the judgment day. Revelation 14 describes judgment day as the destruction of Babylon, which was the spiritual description of Jerusalem. In Hebrews 13:11-14, the writer told the Jews to go outside the camp where Jesus was crucified and to look for the enduring city of the New Jerusalem. This was a clear commandment to leave the city of Jerusalem before it was destroyed in 70AD. Revelation is not confusing, but it is remarkably accurate when we use the Bible to interpret it, instead of being swayed by the traditions of men.

The important thing to realize is **that this book is symbolic and was written by a Jew to the Jewish people living in the Roman Empire**. This is why it referred to Jewish things from the Old Testament, like the key of David, the synagogues of Satan, the doctrine of Balaam and Jezebel. These are things that have no relevance in the 21st century but were well known to the Jews, 2000 years ago. The book of Revelation cannot be interpreted by our personal ideas, but **it is understood by using the Old Testament**. For example, John described Jesus as the Lamb who was slain in Revelation 5:6. Now let's ask ourselves: Is Jesus an actual Lamb or was this symbolic language for the Jews who knew that Christ was the final sacrifice that fulfilled the Law? In Revelation 12:1, John described a woman who gave birth to Christ, and she was standing in heaven, clothed with the sun, moon and stars. Was this a woman literally standing in the sky? The truth is that Genesis 37:9 tells us that **the sun, moon and stars represented Israel** from whom Christ was born.

In Revelation 13, John described a large beast coming out of the sea and another beast from the land. Should we look for monsters coming out of the Pacific Ocean and the underground? Or do we interpret this from Daniel 7 in the Old Testament that tells us that the "beast" was a kingdom that was crushed by God's kingdom in the 1st Century? This clearly indicates that it was talking about Israel and the Pharisees. In the language of the Jews, the "earth" was the "Temple of Israel" that represented their Priesthood and the "sea" was the outer court where the people presented the sacrifices to the priests. **This indicates that the two beasts were the religious leaders of the Temple and the Jewish political rulers at that time.**

Remember that Christ was taken to both beasts when He was crucified. He was first taken to the beast of the sea, represented by King Herod, and finally taken to the beast of the land, represented by the High Priest. Paul also refers to these beasts in Ephesus, as actual people that he fought (1st Corinthians 15:32). From the Bible, we know that Paul's enemies were mainly the Jewish religious leaders. They were also called savage wolves that deceived the believers by using the Law (Acts 20:29-32, Matthew 10:16). Both these religious and political Jewish beasts were destroyed in 70AD by the Roman Empire, which was the army of the Lord (Revelation 19). The kingdom of God represented by Christ the cornerstone, crushed the Jewish beast into pieces in 70AD (Matthew 21:44). At that time, the kingdom of God was transferred from the Jewish beast to the Gentile nations (Matthew 21:43).

John describes Satan as a large dragon in Revelation 12, who accused the Jewish brethren. Was this a spiritual monster or something the Jews understood? The truth is that Jesus symbolically called the Pharisees as the "children of the devil" because they accused their fellow Jewish brethren using the Law of Moses (John 5:45, John 8:3). Satan was the old covenant system of the Pharisees and their accusation using the Law. The bride of Christ, which was the Church of believing Jews, overcame the old covenant system (Satan) by the New Covenant blood of the Lamb (Christ) and their testimony. They were faithful until death, and Christ finally won the battle in 70AD.

*Isaiah 1:1,21 "The vision of Isaiah the son of Amoz, which he saw concerning Judah and **Jerusalem** ... The faithful **city** has become a **prostitute**!"*

The Babylon of Revelation 17 is known as the Great Prostitute and it has been incorrectly applied to the Catholic Church, modern-day Iraq and many other things. But when we use the Bible to interpret itself, we will find that this whore who drank the blood of the saints, was the Pharisees, that Jesus described in Matthew 23:35 – because He said that all the blood of the martyrs would be avenged on the Pharisees. **In Isaiah 1:1,21, we see that Jerusalem is described as a prostitute**. In Romans 7:1-6, Paul tells the Jews that they would be committing spiritual adultery if they returned to their old husband (Law) instead of bearing fruit with their new husband (Christ). James called the Jews as adulterers and enemies of God (James 4:4). We know from Romans 5:9-10 and Romans 4:15, that those under the Law were God's enemies who were going to face His wrath. We were never adulterers or enemies of God because we were never under the Old Covenant. In Jeremiah 51, God called the Old Testament Jews to come out of Babylon before the Persians destroyed the city. In the same way, God called the New Testament Jews to leave Jerusalem (Babylon) before it was destroyed by fire in 70AD (Revelation 18:4-8). The 144,000 from Revelation 7 are not the Jehovah Witnesses or any Christians today because it was referring to the full number of Jewish believers who escaped Jerusalem when they were sealed with the Holy Spirit. This is because we see the same language describing the sealing of the Jews before the destruction of Jerusalem by the Babylonians in the Old Testament (Ezekiel 9:4).

The mark of the beast is not a microchip, credit card, smartphone or anything in the 21st century. It was something that was relevant to the people of the 1st Century. The believers were sealed with the Holy Spirit, but the unbelieving Jews received the mark of the beast in their forehead or right hand. This was symbolic language that described the Jews worshipping their political leaders who fought against the Romans. Remember that the Jews refused to worship Christ when they found out that He did not come to destroy the Romans but that He came to destroy the Temple and take away the Law & their religion. Jesus actually told the Jews to pay taxes to Caesar instead of rebelling against Rome. The Jews wanted their kingdom to be established in Jerusalem and worshiped anyone who promised that. This false promise was made by the false Jewish Messiah and the political leaders. But the believers obeyed Christ's words and refused to worship the beast, but endured persecution and escaped Jerusalem before the Romans destroyed it.

Just as the Old Testament Jews were forced to worship the image of King Nebuchadnezzar or lose their lives in Daniel 3, in the same way, the New Testament Jews were forced to buy and sell only if they worshiped the beast, or else they would lose their lives. **The mark of the beast meant that the Jews worshiped the old covenant system**. This is why John warned everyone in the 1st Century not to add or remove from the Book of Revelation because it contained crucial instructions about the end times for the Churches in Asia. If someone had modified his letter to those seven churches in Asia, then they may have worshiped the beast or fallen away due to persecution. It has absolutely nothing to do with us today. Today even if people misunderstand the book of Revelation, we cannot lose our salvation. We don't have to worry about the spirit of Jezebel or the synagogue of Satan because those were referring to the Pharisees and the Old Covenant ministry that passed away. We don't have to worry about the mark of the beast or the antichrist because the Roman Empire destroyed the Temple in 70AD and the Pharisees don't exist today. **The Book of Revelation was fulfilled more than 1900 years ago!**

The seven seals of Revelation 6 are not about the future, but they were about the events of Matthew 24 that culminated in the destruction of Jerusalem. The four horsemen of doom were not about futuristic events, but Jeremiah 15 describes them as four types of sufferings experienced by the city of Jerusalem. The seven woes of Revelation are nothing but the seven times Jesus pronounced woe upon the Pharisees in Matthew 23. This was fulfilled during the great tribulation and the final judgment of 70AD when the Temple was destroyed in Matthew 24 & 25. In Revelation 8, a third of the earth is supposedly destroyed, but the true interpretation is found in Ezekiel 5 that talks about the destruction of a third of the city of Jerusalem. When the Bible said that the elect would be taken from the four corners of heaven, we will find that Ezekiel 7 and Revelation 7 talk about the people being saved from the four corners of the land of Israel and not the entire world. The war of Armageddon was already fought between the Jewish beasts and the Roman armies in 70AD and this has nothing to do with modern-day Israel.

The Book of Revelation is not about the end of the world, but it was about the end of the Old Covenant where old things passed away in 70AD when Jerusalem was destroyed. **It was the revelation of the New Covenant** where God made all things new by no longer imputing sin to the world. It was the revelation of a New Jerusalem – a spiritual city where God did not dwell in a Temple separated from the people by the priesthood, but where God lives in every one of us.

*Isaiah 25:7-9 NASB "on this mountain He will **swallow up the covering** which is over all peoples, Even the **veil** which is stretched over all nations. He will swallow up **death** for all time, And the Lord GOD will wipe tears away from all faces, **And He will remove the reproach of His people from all the earth;** For the LORD has spoken. And it will be said in that day, "**Behold, this is our God for whom we have waited that He might save us.** This is the LORD for whom we have waited; Let us rejoice and be glad in **His salvation**."*

The book of Revelation was about the removal of the veil of the Law that blinded all people (2nd Corinthians 3:12-18, 4:3-4). The Law was the ministry of spiritual death (2nd Corinthians 3:7). By removing the Law, **Christ removed spiritual death from all people**. This happened when **Christ was revealed through the destruction of the Temple**. This was the revelation of Grace through Christ's 2nd coming. The salvation of Christ was announced on the Cross and was fully revealed in 70AD.

Resurrection and Judgment Day in 70AD

*Daniel 12:1-2,7 "**At that time** shall Michael stand up, the great prince who stands for the children of **your people**; and there shall **be a time of trouble**, such as never was since there was a nation even to that same time: and at that time your people shall be delivered, everyone who shall be found written in the book. Many of those who sleep in the dust of the earth shall awake, some to everlasting life, and some to shame and everlasting contempt ... when they have finished **breaking in pieces the power of the holy people, all these things shall be finished**."*

The people of Israel looked forward to the resurrection of the dead during the time of great tribulation that was predicted by Christ in Matthew 24:21, when the Temple was about to be destroyed in 70AD. That was the time when the power of the Jews was destroyed because they refused to trust in Christ but trusted in the power of their Temple and priestly system.

Ezekiel 24:21 "Behold, I will profane my sanctuary (temple), the pride of your power, the desire of your eyes"

Daniel was told to seal the prophecy till the Jews would increase in knowledge in the "end times" (Daniel 12:4). It was not talking about the increase of technology or civilization, but the increased knowledge of the prophecies among the Jews. This happened at the time of Christ when He revealed the Gospel to the Jews by announcing the kingdom. This was continued by the Apostles who preached to all the Jews in the Roman Empire. When John wrote Revelation, the Lord told him that the time had finally come for the resurrection and judgment of the dead. It was the time when the prophecy of Daniel was unsealed and fulfilled.

Revelation 22:10,12 **"Don't seal up the words of the prophecy of this book, for the time is at hand** ... *Behold I come quickly. My reward is with me to repay each man according to his work"*

The resurrection was for all those under the Old Covenant when their works would be judged. The spirits of those who died under the Law were asleep and waiting for the 2nd coming of Christ so that they were resurrected into His presence. They were trapped in the body of spiritual death as Paul writes here:

Romans 7:1-2, 24-25 "Or don't you know, brothers (for I speak to men who know the law), that the law has dominion over a man for as long as he lives? ... Who will deliver me out of the body of this death? I thank God through Jesus Christ, our Lord!"

They were trapped in a spiritual place called Hades and were eagerly waiting to be released from the Law by the resurrection in 70AD. They had the promise of resurrection when they received the Holy Spirit in their lives. Just as Jesus was raised from the dead, they too would be resurrected in 70AD.

Romans 8:11"But if the Spirit of him who raised up Jesus from the dead dwells in you, he who raised up Christ Jesus from the dead will also give life to your mortal bodies through his Spirit who dwells in you."

There were two resurrections in Revelation 20. The first one was for the martyrs who gave up their lives by not going back to the Old Covenant system. These were the Disciples of Christ who carried the cross and gave up their lives for Him. Only those who suffered with Him in death would be glorified with Him and reign with Him for a 1000 years (Romans 8:17, Revelation 20:4-5). Paul was one such person who lost his life as a martyr so that He could partake in this resurrection.

Philippians 3:10-11 "that I may know him, and the power of his resurrection, and the fellowship of his sufferings, becoming conformed to his death; if by any means I may attain to the resurrection"

Paul and the saints were eagerly waiting for this resurrection in their lifetime.

*Galatians 5:5 NIV "For through the Spirit we **eagerly** await by faith the righteousness for which we hope"*

*Philippians 3:20-21 NASB "For our citizenship is in heaven, from which also we **eagerly** wait for a Savior, the Lord Jesus Christ who will transform the body of our humble state"*

When Christ returned in 70AD, the martyrs received their resurrection of glory and reigned with Christ for 1000 years. This was not a literal thousand-year period on earth because the Bible never talks about such a period in the entire Old Testament. The only place this is mentioned is in Revelation, which is a symbolic book. Christ began to reign at the time of His resurrection, and His kingdom has no end (Matthew 28:18, Isaiah 9:7). The 1000 years was a spiritual duration of time in the heavenly realms where the martyrs received great glory to reign with Christ. The 1000 years in heaven were like one day to the Lord on earth. The martyrs reigned with Christ for 1000 spiritual years that ended in 70AD, but Christ's reign continues forever and ever. The binding of Satan was the destruction of Jerusalem and the Pharisees in the Temple. Shortly after this event, the Church was persecuted by the Jewish ministers of Satan (Law), who were scattered in all the nations (Luke 21:44). The Jews living in all nations attacked the Church throughout the Roman Empire until they were also destroyed. This spiritual war was the War of Gog and Magog (Revelation 20:8), where Christ finally defeated the enemies of His Church in the 1st Century.

At the time of His 2nd coming, the general resurrection of the dead took place for all the rest of the people under the Old Covenant. Both the resurrections were completed in 70AD and they were spiritual in nature. The resurrected spiritual body was not the same as the earthly body. The earthly body was flesh and blood, but the spiritual body was heavenly and cannot be seen now. Paul says that the people under the Law would not remain asleep forever but would be raised from spiritual death. They were dead under the Law in Hades, separated from God until the final trumpet.

*1st Corinthians 15:52-57 "For the trumpet will sound, and the dead will be raised incorruptible, and we will be changed. For this perishable body must become imperishable, and this mortal must put on immortality. But when this perishable body will have become imperishable, and this mortal will have put on immortality, then what is written will happen: "Death is swallowed up in victory." "Death, where is your sting? Hades, where is your victory？" "The sting of death is sin, and the **power of sin is the law**. But thanks be to God, who gives us the victory through our Lord Jesus Christ."*

The final trumpet was blown in Jerusalem when the city was destroyed (Joel 2:1). In Revelation 11, it clearly says that Jerusalem would be trampled for 42 months, and this matches Matthew 24, Luke 21 and Daniel 12:7. All these scriptures clearly show that the Roman siege of Jerusalem that lasted exactly 42 months until 70AD was the time of the Resurrection. It was at that time that Christ crushed the final enemy of "spiritual death" that was caused by the Law. When Christ removed the Temple, the Law passed away, and this removed the power of the Law – which was spiritual death. Christ raised the dead and destroyed Hades forever. There was no more spiritual death or separation from God. **The final judgment in 70AD was according to their works** (Revelation 20:12) because the Law imputed sins based on works. Today we are past the judgment because we are in the New Covenant. **We will never be judged because we were not born in sin under the Old Covenant that passed away in 70AD.** Today we live in the New Covenant, and we are not separated from the Father. When we live, He is with us. When we die, our spirits go back to the Lord, and we are with Him forever. This is why we say that people who passed away are with the Lord. They are not waiting for a resurrection anymore because we do not live in the body of spiritual death under the Law. We have eternal life both on this earth and in heaven when we die.

All things are new

*Revelation 21:3-6 "he will dwell with them, and they will be his people, and God himself will be with them as their God. He will wipe away from them every tear from their eyes. Death will be no more; neither will there be mourning, nor crying, nor pain, any more. The first things have passed away." He who sits on the throne said, **"Behold, I am making all things new."** He said, "Write, for these words of God are faithful and true." He said to me, "It is DONE! I am the Alpha and the Omega, the Beginning and the End"*

At the end of 70AD, God declared that humanity is living in a new heaven and earth in the New Covenant. The old covenant system that was also known as the old heaven and earth finally passed away with the destruction of the Temple and the resurrection of the dead. God made a new covenant where the old things would not be remembered anymore. There is no more Temple, sacrifice for sin or priesthood because Jesus has made a New Covenant and He lives in and among us forever.

Isaiah 43:18-19 "Don't remember the former things, and don't consider the things of old. Behold, I will do a new thing."

God is telling the world today to forget the Law. He is telling us that sin has been taken away. He is declaring that the judgment and wrath are over. We are living in the New Covenant where God does not impute sin anymore. We are all righteous and sinless in Christ. Now that does not mean that we live in a perfect world without death or suffering. In Isaiah 65:17-22, it talks about the new heaven and earth where people live & die, build homes and do their work. This is referring to the world we live in ever since 70AD.

Revelation 21 was not talking about the absence of physical death or suffering in the new heaven and earth. It was talking about the end of spiritual pain and death. In the Old Covenant, Jerusalem was a place of judgment, death and sorrow in 70AD. The unbelieving Jews faced the wrath and were spiritually separated from God. But today, we live in the New Jerusalem, where there is no more judgment, and therefore there is no more spiritual death, sorrow and pain. From a physical point of view, when we leave this earth, there is no more physical death or pain or tears, but we are with the Lord forever. **We are with the Lord in both this life and after death.** His presence is in us and with us. So in this way Revelation is fulfilled. All of humanity has been restored.

Some may say that there is still so much evil in this world, but if we compare life in the 21st Century to the time of Christ, then we are very fortunate to be alive now. **The world was a horrible place 2000 years ago.** In those days, the Church was persecuted by the Jews throughout the world and almost became extinct. Today due to religious freedom, the Church has grown to 2.3 billion people, and members of all faiths enjoy religious freedom in most countries with decreasing persecution every year. Slavery and racism were common many years ago, but today they are being eradicated from society. Human rights have advanced so greatly that women are CEOs, presidents & leaders with equal rights in most nations. Diseases have dramatically reduced in the last 1000 years. Cures are being discovered in every generation. Scientists will reverse aging in the next century. The average life expectancy has doubled in the last 300 years. Infant mortality has decreased by 95% in the last 200 years. The quality of life has improved dramatically due to technological and social advances. Democracy is common today, with dictators and evil regimes falling in every generation. **The world is a far better place than it was 100, 500 and 2000 years ago.** The world will never end because God will never stop having children. His kingdom will never end (Isaiah 9:7) but will continue to cover the entire earth (Isaiah 11:9) from generation to generation (Psalm 100:5). In the Old Covenant there was a "last day" in 70AD, but in the New Covenant, there are no "last days" because it is an everlasting covenant where God will never judge us and never stops doing good to us (Jeremiah 32:40)

Revelation 22:1-5 "He showed me a river of water of life, clear as crystal, proceeding out of the throne of God and of the Lamb, in the middle of its street. On this side of the river and on that was the tree of life, bearing twelve kinds of fruits, yielding its fruit every month. The leaves of the tree were for the healing of the nations. There will be no curse any more. The throne of God and of the Lamb will be in it, and his servants serve him. They will see his face, and his name will be on their foreheads. There will be no night, and they need no lamp light; for the Lord God will illuminate them. They will reign forever and ever."

In the New Covenant, the presence of God is with us always. The river of life is not a real river, but it is the Holy Spirit within us. Remember how Jesus said in John 7:38 that the Spirit was like rivers of living water within us. The tree of life is Christ Himself, and we are the branches because He lives in us. There are no more curses because the Law and the judgment have passed away. There is no more separation due to the Law, so now all men can see the face of God by knowing His unconditional love that keeps no record of wrongs. They will not need the "light" of the sun, moon, stars of Israel and its Old Covenant system anymore but the Good News of Christ is the light to the nations. Under the Old Covenant, the Jews preached the Law in all the nations, and this brought division and hostility between Jew and Gentile. It was because the Jews alone were God's people and the Gentiles were unclean. The Law divided humanity. But Christ removed the Law and the hostility between the Jew and Gentile by making them a new creation.

*Ephesians 2:13-16 NASB "But now in Christ Jesus you who formerly were far off (Gentile) have been brought near by the blood of Christ. For **He Himself is our peace, who made both groups (Jew and Gentile) into one** and broke down the barrier of the dividing wall, **by abolishing in His flesh the enmity, which is the Law** of commandments contained in ordinances, so that in Himself He might* *make the two into one new man, thus establishing peace, and might **reconcile** them both in one **body** to God through the cross"*

*Isaiah 11:1,6,12 NIV "A shoot will come up from the stump of Jesse; from his roots a Branch will bear fruit ... **The wolf will live with the lamb**...and a little child will lead them ... He will raise a banner for the **nations** and gather the exiles of **Israel**;"*

The "wolf" and the "lamb" living together was referring to the removal of the Law between Jew and Gentile as Paul wrote in Romans 11:10-12. Both Jew and Gentile were sinners under the Old Covenant. But now in Christ, we have all become righteous and united as a new humanity where there is no Jew or Gentile and no more sinners. In Matthew 24:14, Jesus said that the "end" would come when the Gospel was fully preached to all nations. He had sent the Jewish apostles starting at Jerusalem, Judea, Samaria and to the ends of the known Roman world. The Gospel was preached by Paul throughout the Old Covenant world by first going to the Jew and then to the Greek converts. He always went first to the synagogue to preach to the Jews and when they rejected it; he turned to the non-Jews. The Gospel was about receiving salvation from the wrath of the Law. At some time before 70AD, Paul had finished preaching the Gospel.

*Colossians 1:23 NIV "This is the gospel that you heard and that **has been proclaimed to <u>every</u> creature under heaven**, and of which I, Paul, have become a servant."*

*Romans 15:19 "from Jerusalem, and around as far as to Illyricum, I have **<u>fully</u> preached** the Good News of Christ;"*

When the Gospel was fully preached in the Old Covenant world, then came the "end" of the Age of the Law in 70AD. At that time God had made a New Covenant where there is no more Law or judgment. So now, we should not be preaching a Gospel of salvation from the wrath, because the judgment is over. The Gospel for today is that Jesus has saved all of humanity by making a New Covenant where all people are righteous. God sees no difference between Jew and non-Jew, between Christian and non-Christian. This message brings healing to the nations by bringing the gospel of peace, grace and love. It heals every man-made division because now through Christ there is no male or female, no Jew or Gentile, no difference in religion, no difference in riches or social status or sexual orientation.

Colossians 2:16-17 NLT "So don't let anyone condemn you for what you eat or drink, or for not celebrating certain holy days or new moon ceremonies or Sabbaths.

For these rules are only shadows of the reality yet to come. And **Christ himself is that reality**"

What about Israel today? Ever since Israel became a nation in 1948, the Christian world has been making predictions about the return of Christ. Even today, there is a great focus on blood moons, Shemitahs, Jewish calendars, etc. But Paul told the Church that all these Old Covenant "shadows" were passing away. The reality is found in Christ, and He removed the Old Covenant in 70AD to make a New Covenant where there is no more Jew or Gentile. God's holy land is not the nation of Israel because you and I are the promised land. We are the holiest place because Christ lives in us. We are "Christ in us, the glory of God" (Colossians 1:27, 2nd Corinthians 4:4-6). God does not live in Jerusalem, but He has made us the New Jerusalem. Under the Old Covenant, Israel built two Temples that were destroyed. But then Christ came as the true Temple of God who defeated death. After his death and resurrection, His presence lives in us to make us the final Temple that will never be destroyed but endures from generation to generation. We are the Body of Christ. He will not live in a lifeless temple building in Jerusalem because He has found his resting place in us.

Daniel 9:24 NASB "Seventy weeks have been decreed for your people and your holy city, to finish the transgression, to make an end of sin, to make atonement for iniquity, to bring in everlasting righteousness, to seal up vision and prophecy and to anoint the most holy place."

Daniel prophesied that there would be 490 years given to Israel for Jesus to come and bring salvation. But unfortunately, we have introduced a 2000-year gap in the last seven years of that prophecy. We hear that God will one day resume the "clock" and bring the end times with Christ's 2nd coming. The good news is that the Bible clearly shows that 490 years was fulfilled exactly from the time of Jerusalem being rebuilt after their Babylonian exile. During those 490 years, Jesus came and died on the cross to take away sins. **In His 2nd coming, He brought everlasting righteousness to humanity by taking away the Law and anointing us as the "Holy Place".** When Israel was destroyed in 70AD, it was the last curse under the Old Covenant (Malachi 4:6). It was the end of God's wrath (Revelation 15:1). God has given the world great evidence that He has forgiven Israel, by allowing them to be restored to their land. God loves all nations the same – both Arabs and Israelis are His children through Jesus Christ. Today the focus should not be on Israel, the "holy land", "Armageddon war" or "antichrist" but it should be on Jesus Christ who has finished the work. The good news is that the event of 70AD was the War of Armageddon that witnessed the 2nd coming of Christ and the destruction of the antichrist system of the Old

Covenant. When this truth is known, then the world will realize that the holy land is not a country but that we have all been made holy in Christ. Then there will be peace and healing in all nations.

Relax, the "End times is over."

Chapter 4

No more fear

God is love, and there is no fear in love. But so much of religion is driven by the fear of punishment. So many Christians relate to God based on fear. I used to be like many believers who served God out of fear rather than knowing the Father's love. Most of this fear is based on an incorrect understanding of the Bible. I hope the knowledge of the truth will set us free.

The broad road to destruction was for Israel

When I preached a sermon at my Church in 2008, I quoted Matthew 7:21 warning my fellow believers that Jesus was coming soon and that not everyone who called Him "Lord, Lord", would go to heaven. I told them that the broad majority of Christians would go to hell, but only the narrow minority of very devoted Christians would be saved. I told them to stop sinning and surrender their lives because the judgment was coming. But when I understood the context many years later, I was set free from this fear-based teaching.

Luke 13:22-29 *"He went on his way through cities and villages, teaching, and traveling on to **Jerusalem**. One said to him, "Lord, are they few who are saved?" He said to them, "**Strive to enter in by the narrow door**, for many, I tell you, will seek to enter in, and will not be able. When once the master of the house has risen up, and has shut the door, and you begin to stand outside, and to knock at the door, saying, '**Lord, Lord, open to us!**' then he will answer and tell you, 'I don't know you or where you come from.' **Then you will begin to say, 'We ate and drank in your presence, and you taught in our streets.'** He will say, 'I* *tell you, I don't know where you come from. Depart from me, all you workers of iniquity.' There will be weeping and gnashing of teeth, when you see Abraham, Isaac, Jacob, and all the prophets, in God's Kingdom, and yourselves being thrown outside. They will come from the east, west, north, and south, and will sit down in God's Kingdom."*

Jesus preached in Israel and called His disciples to forsake the Law and sell all their possessions to leave Jerusalem before it was destroyed in 70AD. When Jesus spoke to the Jews, He was telling them that the broad majority of Jews would not believe in Him. But only a narrow minority of them would be saved. Jesus was not talking to any of us because it says that those who were left out would tell Him that they personally ate with Him and heard His teaching. This clearly shows that this was about the Jews who personally witnessed Christ and not anyone else. During the 2nd coming of Christ, most of the Jews perished in Jerusalem in 70AD, but most of the Gentiles from all other nations were saved.

The Parables have been fulfilled

Every generation of Christianity thinks that they need to be the wise virgins, the sheep or the faithful servants who need to be prepared for Christ's 2nd coming. But for 2000 years, nothing has happened. So then, what were the parables describing? Jesus told his disciples about the kingdom of God but spoke in parables to the unbelieving Jews (Mark 4:11). This was because the kingdom was going to be taken away from Israel and given to the rest of the world.

Matthew 21:43-45 "God's Kingdom will be taken away from you, and will be given to a nation producing its fruit. He who falls on this stone will be broken to pieces, but on whomever it will fall, it will scatter him as dust." **When the chief priests and the Pharisees heard his parables, they perceived that he spoke about them."**

The Bible tells you this glorious truth – **every single parable in the Bible was about the Pharisees**. It was all about the destruction of Jerusalem in 70AD.

The parable of the sower and the seed was about the gospel being preached in Israel. Most of the Jews heard the Gospel but preferred to believe the message of the Pharisees instead. Some of the Jews believed but went back to the Law due to the persecution from the Pharisees. Some other Jews believed but were so busy with their jobs, families and the worries of life, that they did not leave Jerusalem when it was destroyed. Only a small minority of Jews overcame unbelief, persecution and the love of their possessions to leave Jerusalem and be saved from the wrath of 70AD.

Why can we be so sure that the parables were all about the destruction of Jerusalem in 70AD? It's because the Bible clearly indicates it here:

*Matthew 22:2-3, 5-7 "**The Kingdom of Heaven is like a certain king, who made a marriage feast for his son**, and sent out his servants to call those who were invited to the marriage feast, but they would not come ... they made light of it, and went their ways, one to his own farm, another to his merchandise, and the rest grabbed his servants, and treated them shamefully, and killed them. **When the king heard that, he was angry, and sent his armies, destroyed those murderers, and burned their city.**"*

This parable of the marriage feast or **wedding banquet** was clearly about the Jews who were invited by Christ and the apostles, but they refused for various reasons. The Jews crucified Christ and killed the apostles. But in the end, God the Father (the King) sent His armies (Roman Empire) and destroyed those murderers by burning the city of Jerusalem in 70AD. The wedding banquet took place during Christ's 2nd coming when the saints were resurrected. Today we are always feasting with the Lord because He lives in us.

When Jesus spoke to His disciples about His 2nd coming within their generation, He spoke in three parables. The first one was **the parable of the talents**. Now, I have heard many believers who think that their "talent" is their money, career, hobbies, gifts, skills, etc. They are afraid that if they are not faithful, then they will lose salvation. But we will find that the "talent" here was not any of those, but it was the Gospel given to the Apostles.

*Matthew 25:14,19 "For it is like a man, going into another country, who called his own servants, and **entrusted his goods to them** ... Now after a long time the lord of those servants **came, and reconciled accounts with them**"*

First of all, we notice that the Lord came to settle accounts to the same disciples to whom He gave the talents. So the 2nd coming of the Lord was to those whom He first preached to – the Jews, and not us. Now here is the clinching evidence. Did Jesus give them money? In another account of the same event, we will find that He told them not to take any money but only to preach.

*Matthew 10:5-7,9,23 "**Jesus sent these twelve** out, and commanded them, saying, "Don't go among the Gentiles, and don't enter into any city of the Samaritans.*

*Rather, **go to the lost sheep of the house of Israel**. As you go, **preach….Don't take any gold**, silver, or brass in your money belts … when they persecute you in this city, flee into the next, for most certainly I tell you, **you will not have gone through the cities of Israel, until the Son of Man has come.***"

It is crystal clear that Jesus gave this "talent" to the 12 Apostles. The talent was not money, but it was the Gospel. They were sent without any money and preached only to the Jews. His coming to settle the accounts would happen before they finished preaching in Israel. This happened in 70AD.

Then next parable was **the parable of the virgins.** Now many Christians are told to be "ready" by having enough "oil" in their lamps, supposedly by being regular to Church and serving actively in some form. We think that the "oil" represents the Holy Spirit. But was Jesus even speaking to us?

*Matthew 25:1 "**Then** the Kingdom of Heaven will be like ten virgins, who took their lamps, and went out to meet the bridegroom"*

The time context of this parable is crucial. Jesus said that the kingdom would be like ten virgins at a specific time. When was that time? If we read the Bible in context, we will find that Matthew 24 talks about the destruction of the Temple in 70AD. At that time the Jews were called to leave Jerusalem to meet the bridegroom. But some of them were not ready, and they went back to the city and were trapped. It says that when the Lord came, the "door" was shut. History shows that when the Romans surrounded Jerusalem, the believers escaped the city. But the unbelieving Jews remained in the city for some more time. After a while, the Romans attacked one final time, and they shut down the doors of the city so that nobody could escape. The Jews who perished in the city in 70AD were the foolish virgins. This language of the oil, virgins, and lamps was specific to the Jewish culture. In the Jewish tradition, the bridegroom goes away from the bride after being engaged. He will go and prepare his home with his father and suddenly come with a loud trumpet and take the bride into the wedding feast. The virgins were those who accompanied the bride as she goes to meet her husband. If they were not prepared for the wedding feast, then they would not be allowed to enter it. All this was talking about the preparation of the Jews for the event of 70AD. It has nothing to do with us. We are already one with Christ, and no man can shut the door that He has opened to us.

The last parable in the same chapter of Matthew 25 is **the parable of the sheep and the goats.** Many people think that this is in the future, but Matthew 16:28 and Matthew 10:23 clearly state that Christ's 2nd coming and judgment would happen when the apostles were still preaching in Israel before all of them died. Today, many Christians have served in various ministries hoping to be the "sheep", yearning to hear the words "well done faithful servant". But who were these sheep and goats? If you remember, Christ had called the Jews as the lost sheep of Israel. He had never named any gentiles as sheep. They were considered as outsiders. Jesus told the Jews that those who believed in Him would be like the sheep who heard his voice. But those Jews who did not believe in Him would be like the goats. The "least of these" were not the homeless and poor people we see today, but it was the apostles themselves.

*1st Corinthians 4:9,11 "For, I think, God has exhibited us **apostles last of all, as men** ... To this present hour we are both hungry and thirsty, and are poorly clothed, and are roughly treated, and are homeless"*

Jesus told the Jews that if they welcomed the Apostles and even gave them a drink of water, then they would not lose their reward in heaven (Matthew 10:42). **The judgment of the sheep and goats was about Israel and how they treated the apostles.** Those who believed the Gospel loved the apostles, but the unbelievers ignored and persecuted the apostles. The sheep followed the Lord and heard his voice when He called them out of Jerusalem before it was destroyed, but the goats perished in the city in 70AD. Today we are not the sheep or the goat, but we are one with Christ. You don't need to tithe or help any Christian ministry to go to heaven, because heaven came down into you, by grace without any of your works. *All of the parables were about the Jews that were fulfilled in 70AD.*

The Day of the Lord – Judgment Day is over

The Jewish believers knew that the Day of the Lord was coming soon in their generation. But the unbelieving Jews in Jerusalem were caught by surprise.

1st Thessalonians 5:1-4 "But concerning the times and the seasons, brothers, you have no need that anything be written to you. For you yourselves know well that the day of the Lord comes like a thief in the night. For when they are saying, "Peace and safety," then sudden destruction will come on them, like birth pains on a pregnant woman; and they will in no way escape. But you, brothers, aren't in darkness, that the day should overtake you like a thief."

The Jews of that generation were foolishly thinking that they would have peace in Jerusalem. But just like the Jews in the Old Testament times were suddenly destroyed when the Babylonian armies attacked their city, the

2nd coming of Christ came like a thief in the night and destroyed Jerusalem in 70AD. For more information, please read Ezekiel 7:25, Matthew 24:43, Revelation 3:3 and Revelation 16:15.

The Day of the Lord that came like a thief in the night was coming upon the generation of those seven Churches in Asia.

Revelation 2:12,16, NLT "To the church in Pergamum ... I will come to you suddenly and fight against them with the sword of my mouth"

Revelation 3:1,3,10 NASB "To the angel of the church in Sardis write: ... If you don't wake up, I will come to you suddenly, as unexpected as a thief.... the hour of trial that is going to come on the whole world"

That was the time of great tribulation and the Day of the Lord. When John wrote his epistle, he told them to be ready for the day of judgment (1st John 4:17)

This day came when Christ appeared in the clouds over Israel. The city of Jerusalem in the land of Israel was the spiritual Babylon that was destroyed on the Judgment Day of 70AD.

Revelation 14:7,14,15,19,20 "for the hour of his judgment has come ... Babylon the great has fallen ... I looked, and behold, a white cloud; and on the cloud one sitting like a son of man ... for the harvest of the earth (land of Israel) is ripe ... The angel thrust his sickle into the earth, and gathered the vintage of the earth, and threw it into the great wine press of the wrath of God. The wine press was trodden outside of the city"

Peter spoke about the day of the Lord that would come like a thief in the night to destroy the old heaven and earth and melt its elements by fire in 2nd Peter 3:10. He was not referring to the destruction of the planet but the land of Israel, which was referred to as the old heaven and earth in the language of the Jews. We see this same language used by the prophet Nahum in the destruction of the city of Nineveh by the Babylonians in the old testament, proving that the judgment day was not a global event, but local to Jerusalem.

*Nahum 1:1-3,5-6,8 NIV "A prophecy concerning Nineveh ... The Lord takes vengeance on his foes and vents his wrath against his enemies ... His way is in the storm, and clouds are the dust of his feet ... The mountains quake before him and the hills **melt** away ... His wrath is poured out like **fire**; the rocks are shattered before him ... he will make an end of NINEVEH"*

In the same way, the prophet Elijah would come before the judgment fell on the land of Israel. The sign for that event would be the return of the prophet Elijah.

Malachi 4:5-6 NLT "Look, I am sending you the prophet Elijah before the great and dreadful day of the LORD arrives. His preaching will turn the hearts of fathers to their children, and the hearts of children to their fathers. Otherwise I will come and strike the land with a curse."

But the Jews did not recognize him because it was John the Baptist who came in the spirit of Elijah.

Matthew 17:12-13 NLT "But I tell you, Elijah has already come, but he wasn't recognized, and they chose to abuse him. And in the same way they will also make the Son of Man suffer." Then the disciples realized he was talking about John the Baptist."

We saw that John the Baptist was warning the Pharisees about fleeing from the day of judgment, that would fall on the land of Israel in 70AD (Matthew 3:7,10). The day of judgment was in 70AD when the land of Israel was burnt with fire. We do not live in the days of Elijah, and we are not looking forward to the Day of Judgment. We live in the days of the everlasting grace of Christ, where there is no more judgment.

Rewards at the judgment seat of Christ

Revelation 22:12 "Behold, I come quickly. My reward is with me, to repay to each man according to his work"

Paul preached to the Jew and the Gentile about the judgment seat of Christ that was going to happen soon in their lifetime. This was because the Law imputed sins under the old covenant and both Jew and Gentile were sinners. **This final judgment happened in 70AD, and it was according to works**. The reason it was under works was that all of humanity was under the Old Creation of Adam where they were under the knowledge of good and evil. They were judged according to the Law and received the reward according to works.

*1st Corinthians 3:13-15 "Each man's work will be revealed. **For the Day will declare it, because it is revealed in fire;** and the fire itself will test what sort of work each man's work is. If any man's work remains which he built on it, he will receive a **reward**. If any man's work is burned, he will suffer loss, but he himself will be saved, but as **through fire**"*

This judgment happened on a specific day in 70AD when the Old Covenant system was destroyed in the fire. At that time, all who trusted in the works of the Law perished in the fire. The Roman armies had destroyed the system of the old covenant throughout the world. The Jews and Gentiles who trusted in the law suffered during that judgment.

Unfortunately, the preaching of a future judgment with rewards has put fear in many Christians. Some passages in Colossians 3:23-25 have been used against those who struggle in their jobs so that they are told to work hard to please God and get a reward. If you hate your job, then God is not calling you to grit your teeth and please Him. He is your Father, and He will give you the desire of your heart. He has gifted you with the skills and the passion for the job that He has prepared. We live in the new covenant age where there is no future judgment or rewards to receive. God has created us to live in freedom as sons who enjoy the inheritance, and not slaves who work for rewards. Today, we are past the judgment because we are living in the New Covenant.

Genesis 15:1 "I am your shield, your very great reward."

We don't look forward to future rewards because God himself is our great reward and shield. God has already rewarded us because Christ lives in us now.

Hell was the burning of Jerusalem in 70AD

The idea of sending people to a burning hell is not humane or civilized. A loving God would never send His creation to be burnt forever in conscious torment. This idea was introduced into the early Church from the Roman pagan culture more than 1000 years ago. The apostle Paul never spoke about hell. But we may say that Jesus preached a lot about hell. The truth is that the word "hell" does not even exist in the original Greek language in the Bible. The word is "Gehenna" or the valley of Ben Hinnom, and it was a place outside of Jerusalem. Both hell and the lake of fire referred to this "Gehenna" that was a place where the Jews burnt their animal sacrifices (Hebrews 13:11). When Christ died on the cross, the sacrifice of the Law was coming to an end. But the Jews held on to the Law and its animal sacrifices. Jesus told the Jews that if they wanted to be righteous by trying to keep the Ten Commandments (Law), then they would go to Gehenna (Matthew 5:20-30). Jesus was telling them that Jerusalem would become like a burning fire of Gehenna and that they would perish there along with the sacrifices of the Law. The truth is that Jesus preached about heaven ten times more than He did about Gehenna, showing that He preached much more on grace than on judgment. This "Gehenna" was also the place where the rebellious Jews burnt sacrifices in the fire to their false God "Molech" (Jeremiah 32:35) in the Old Testament. God judged them by making the city of Jerusalem like the "Valley of Ben Hinnom" (Jeremiah 7:30-34). This happened when the Babylonian army burnt the city of Jerusalem. The land was ruined, and all the joy and laughter was replaced with weeping and gnashing of teeth.

History repeated itself when the Roman armies burnt the city of Jerusalem in 70AD during the 2nd coming of Christ. That was how the parable of the wheat and tares was fulfilled when the unbelieving Jews who were thrown into the fire (Matthew 13:41-42). The Jews who were trapped in the city were weeping and gnashing their teeth. This event will never be repeated. But wasn't it an eternal fire in the parable of the sheep and the goats where the devil and his angels were cursed (Matthew 25:41)? This burning fire in Jerusalem was a cursed place for the angels of the devil. The word "angel" means preacher or messenger. The Pharisees were the messengers of Satan who perished in Jerusalem. The curse of the Law fell upon the land of Israel just as it was prophesied in Malachi 4 and confirmed by John the Baptist in Matthew 3.

The word "eternal" does not mean a fire that burns forever and ever, but the original Greek word means "Ending of the Age". The fire of Jerusalem burnt till it finished the Age of the Old Covenant. This is why it was called an unquenchable fire that burnt till it fully removed the Temple, the sacrifices, the Law, the priesthood, the Pharisees and the entire Old Covenant. The fire where the worm did not die was referring to the destruction of Jerusalem in 70AD (Isaiah 66:15,24). We see this concept of a never-ending lake of fire in the Old Testament when Edom was destroyed with sulfur never to be inhabited again with those specific people (Isaiah 34:9-10). We see the same language in Isaiah 30:31-33 that describes the destruction of the Assyrian kingdom in the Old Testament. **Jesus told the Jews that their last days would be like the days of Sodom** when Lot left it, and the city was burnt with fire (Luke 17:28-34). This was fulfilled when the believing Jews fled Jerusalem before 70AD. In Jude 1:7 it says that the city of Sodom was burnt with eternal fire. But we know that the city is not burning today. The meaning of "eternal fire" was that a city like Sodom was judged and burnt once and for all, never to come back again. In the same way, the Old Covenant was destroyed once and for all. There is no more judgment for the Jews or any other nation. The Pharisees and the Old Covenant will never come back again. All the places in the Bible where it says "refiner's fire" or "consuming fire", was about 70AD and will never be repeated.

Today we live in the eternal life of the New Covenant from generation to generation, where God's presence is with us forever (Isaiah 59:21).

The story of Lazarus and the rich man in Luke 16 was not about the burning of the sinners in an eternal fire. It was a parable that Jesus used to describe the judgment of Jerusalem. Lazarus was a symbol of the early Church in Jerusalem, many of whom were poor. This is why Paul made frequent collections for them (Romans 15:26). The rich man was a symbol of the Pharisees who lived by the riches of their Temple and religion. In Luke 16:13-14, it says that the Pharisees were lovers of money and Jesus told them that they could not serve God and money. They had no concern for the poor and persecuted the Church all over the Roman Empire. Revelation 17 and Matthew 23 describe the Pharisees as the rich prostitute who persecuted the poor Church. In 70AD, the Pharisees perished in the fire while the poor believers were saved and united in the resurrection with Abraham and all the righteous saints. I know that people have had visions of hell, but such things are a result of their minds being influenced by wrong teaching from the pulpit and a lack of understanding of God's heart. The "hell" was the wrath of the Law that ended in 70AD. But today the Law has passed away, and we live in never-ending grace. But what about the spirits of the unbelievers who were outside the New Jerusalem?

Revelation 21:8 "But for the cowardly, unbelieving, sinners, abominable, murderers, sexually immoral, sorcerers, idolaters, and all liars, their part is in the lake that burns with fire and sulfur, which is the second death."

The Pharisees were called murderers and liars because they preached the ministry of death (Law) and belonged to their father, the devil who was a murderer and liar (John 8:44). They were also called adulterers because they rejected their true husband (Christ) and went back to the Law (old husband) (Romans 7:1-4, James 4:4). They were called sorcerers because they deceived the believers with their false Gospel of the Law (Galatians 3:1, 2nd Corinthians 11:1-4, Revelation 17:2, 18:23). They perished in the lake of fire in Jerusalem, but their spirits were saved later on. The gates of heaven were open to them (Revelation 21:25, 22:14) and they entered when they finally realized that Jesus is Lord and Savior.

America will not be destroyed

It's a common thing to hear people say that America is going to be destroyed like Sodom because of abortion, gay marriage, etc. They say that the world will be destroyed just like it was judged during Noah's flood. But this is because we don't understand the covenant we live in today. Before 70AD, the entire world was under the tree of the knowledge of good and evil and the Old Covenant. God had no choice but to judge sins because man wanted to be judged by works. The sin of Sodom was not about equal rights for same-sex couples. One of the sins of Sodom was violence where men raped others forcibly (Genesis 19:5). San Francisco and Amsterdam are not the modern-day versions of Sodom! But, the primary sin of Sodom was found here:

Ezekiel 16:49-50 "Behold, this was the iniquity of your sister Sodom: pride, fullness of bread, and prosperous ease was in her and in her daughters; neither did she strengthen the hand of the poor and needy. They were haughty, and committed abomination before me: therefore I took them away when I saw it."

It's interesting how Jerusalem was compared as a sister of Sodom. That's because Jesus said that the Pharisees were the most heartless people, filled with religion but empty of love and compassion. They defended their religion so much that they killed Jesus and the poor people of Israel who believed in Christ. The Pharisees repelled sinners and misfits with their religious rules, but Jesus lived with sinners who were attracted to His love and compassion. The Church should not be judging gays, lesbians and transgender people when it has enough issues of its own. The truth is that we see Christ in atheists and gays who have more compassion and kindness than religious people who only preach about Him. Now, some people will say that this gives us freedom to legalize anything. No, we must be against all forms of abuse and exploitation against men, women and children. The truth is that Christians and atheists, gays and straight, and people of every race and religion, are unanimously against every form of child abuse.

When we look at the people who perished in the flood of Noah, they were filled with constant violence (Genesis 6:11). God had no choice but to protect Noah and his family from that violence and thereby preserve the human race, from whom came Jesus the Savior of the world. Christ said that the last days of 70AD would be like the days of Noah. The Jews were filled with violence, killing the believers and persecuting the Church until 70AD, when the Romans destroyed Jerusalem. Today we live in the New Covenant where God no longer accounts sin and will not judge nations with wrath. But unfortunately many preachers will quote this verse:

2nd Chronicles 7:14 "if my people, who are called by my name, shall humble themselves, and pray, and seek my face, and turn from their wicked ways; then I will hear from heaven, and will forgive their sin, and will heal their land."

This only applied to the Jews who were under the system of works of the Law. They were blessed when they obeyed and cursed when they disobeyed the Law. They had to keep pleading to God, to forgive their sin and heal their land whenever they broke the Law. But today we live in the New Covenant, where God does not impute sin anymore. Our lands have been healed in the name of Jesus because He never sinned.

Worldliness and Riches

When I drive on the roads in America, I have seen bumper stickers saying "NOTW" or "Not of this world". It is very common to hear preachers tell us that we must forsake the world and its patterns. But was it talking about abstaining from secular music, shopping, material pleasures, eating and drinking? Or was it something else? We sing the song "All to Jesus I surrender", declaring that we are going to the Cross by forsaking all worldly pleasures. But what exactly did Paul mean when he said that he died to the world?

Galatians 6:13-15 "For even they who receive circumcision don't keep the law themselves, but they desire to have you circumcised, that they may boast in your flesh. But far be it from me to boast, except in the cross of our Lord Jesus Christ, through which the world has been crucified to me, and I to the world. For in Christ Jesus neither is circumcision anything, nor uncircumcision, but a new creation"

Being crucified to the world was to stop trusting in the Law because of his faith in Jesus Christ's finished work. In Galatians 2:19-21, he said that he had died to the law by trusting in Christ. **The world was the Old Covenant system of righteousness by keeping the Ten Commandments and the Law of Moses.** This is exactly what Jesus told his disciples.

Mark 8:35-38 "For whoever wants to save his life will lose it; and whoever will lose his life for my sake and the sake of the Good News will save it. **For what does it profit a man, to gain the whole world, and forfeit his life?** *For what will a man give in exchange for his life? For whoever will be ashamed of me and of my words in* **this adulterous and sinful generation,** *the Son of Man also will be ashamed of him, when he comes in his Father's glory."*

Jesus told the Jews to believe in Him by giving up their world under the Old Covenant and be persecuted unto death if it was needed. If they tried to preserve their life by going back to the Law, then they would perish in His 2nd coming. All this happened within that generation when the old covenant world passed away. Those who gave up their lives for Christ at the expense of the old covenant world were the ones who received eternal life.

When Jesus died on the cross, it happened at the end of the world. This was the passing away of the Old Covenant system that was known as the Old heaven and earth.

Hebrews 9:26 KJV "but now once in the end of the world hath he appeared to put away sin by the sacrifice of himself."

That is why it said in Hebrews 8:13, that the Old Covenant was soon disappearing in Christ's 2nd coming. That was the end of the world for the Jews. They had to give up their lives and not cling on to the world of the Law, the Temple, and Jerusalem. That is why John told the Jews not to love the world (1st John 2:15). That was also why James told the Jews that they were becoming adulterers by befriending the world (James 4:4, 5:1-2). It's because the Pharisees were lovers of money who loved the riches of the Temple system. They were going back to the riches of the Old Covenant system instead of selling their possessions and fleeing Jerusalem before it was destroyed in 70AD.

*2nd Corinthians 5:16-19 NIV "So from now on we regard no one from a **worldly** (flesh) point of view. Though we once regarded Christ in this way, we do so no longer. Therefore, if anyone is in Christ, the new creation has come: The **old** has gone, the **new** is here! All this is from God, who reconciled us to himself through Christ and gave us the ministry of reconciliation: that God was reconciling the world to himself in Christ, not counting people's sins against them."*

Paul made that remarkable statement that he no longer looked at people from a worldly point of view. **This worldly view was the flesh or the old covenant system that judged people according to their sins.** When we judge people by their works and sins, we are going back to that dead old world system of the Law. But God made all things new by making a New Creation in Christ, where He does not account sins to humanity, but He has made all creation, righteous in Christ. That is what God meant when He said that old things had passed away and all things were new in Revelation 21:4-5. **In 70AD, a New World order was created under the new covenant, where all humanity has been made righteous** without any more judgment of works. Today we are part of this beautiful new world where we can enjoy all the free gifts of life without feeling guilty.

In the old covenant world, the rich Jewish rulers of the Temple were judged because they refused to help the poor believers who had sold their possessions and were following Jesus. They failed to help the least of their brethren.

Hebrews 13:5 "Be free from the love of money, content with such things as you have, for he has said, "I will in no way leave you, neither will I in any way forsake you"

They were called to stop loving their wealth that was concentrated in Jerusalem and its temple, but to leave it by faith in Christ, looking for the New Jerusalem that came in 70AD (Hebrews 13:12-14). Christ told them that even if they had given up the wealth of the Temple, that He would not forsake them.

That is why James told the Jews not to make plans for their life in the city of Jerusalem. He told them to watch and pray because the Lord's coming was near and therefore not to store their riches that were going to be destroyed in the fire of 70AD.

James 4:13-14, 5:2-3,8 "Come now, you who say, "Today or tomorrow let's go into this city, and spend a year there, trade, and make a profit." Whereas you don't know what your life will be like tomorrow ... Your gold and silver are corroded and will eat your flesh like fire. You have laid up your treasure in the last days ... the coming of the Lord is at hand."

This is exactly what Christ said in the parable of the rich Jewish man who made plans to use his money, but suddenly lost his life (Luke 12:16-20). It's because the Jewish world under the old covenant was going to be destroyed, suddenly after 1500 years. **We also see how Christ told the rich young ruler to sell everything and carry the cross to be saved.**

*Matthew 19:21,24-30 "**If you want to be perfect, go, sell what you have, and give to the poor, and you will have treasure in heaven; and come, follow me** ... Again I tell you, it is easier for a camel to go through a needle's eye, than for a rich man to enter into God's Kingdom ... Jesus said to them, "Most certainly I tell you that you who have followed me, in the regeneration when the Son of Man will sit on the throne of his glory, you also will sit **on twelve thrones, judging the twelve tribes of Israel.** Everyone who has left houses, or brothers, or sisters, or father, or mother, or wife, or children, or lands, for my name's sake, will receive one hundred times, and will inherit eternal life. But many will be last who are first; and first who are last."*

It's because he was a rich Pharisee who was trying to be righteous by keeping the Law. He had great riches, due to the Jewish religion and Temple. When Jesus told him to be perfect by selling all his possessions, this was similar to the call found in Matthew 5:48, where the Jews were commanded to fulfill the Law by becoming as perfect as God, by even loving their enemies. This is why Christ told the Jews to fulfill the Law by loving God with all their heart, soul and strength, by loving Him more than money and selling all their possessions to leave Jerusalem, before it was destroyed. The disciples had obeyed this commandment and were saved from the wrath of 70AD. They gave up their lives and reigned with Him in the resurrection. As you can see, **it was related only to the judgment of the 12 tribes of Israel that happened in 70AD**. This call is not for us today because we were never under the Law. God loved us first with all his heart, soul and strength in saving us. We enjoy money because God loves us and gives it as a gift. We are not commanded to sell our possessions or leave Jerusalem because we live in the New Covenant post-70AD. Christ is not testing us by asking us to give up our desires. He is not asking us to become perfect by selling everything because **He sold everything and died on the cross to make us perfect forever.** We don't have to move a muscle because Christ did everything for us and finished the work.

Today we can eat, drink and enjoy life because God has removed the law and given us free gifts! **Today it is not a sin to be rich or love money or the pleasures of life**. It is easy for us to criticize the millionaires and billionaires and say that they are too rich. Remember that we are always richer than someone else who is in a worse financial condition and they can also judge us for being too rich. In the New Covenant world, there is no sin and being rich is not a sin. All these are free gifts from God to be enjoyed. It is the love of God within our heart that causes us to share our blessings with those who are less fortunate. Jesus gave up His life on the Cross and destroyed the Old Covenant system of judgment so that we can enjoy the abundant life right here and now.

Doctrine of demons

It is common to hear a lot about demons and Satan in some Christian denominations. I was always rebuking Satan and casting out demons from my problems. But what was this doctrine of demons?

1st Timothy 4:1-4 NLT "Now the Holy Spirit tells us clearly that in the last times some will turn away from the true faith; they will follow deceptive spirits and teachings that come from demons. These people are hypocrites and liars, and their consciences are dead. They will say it is wrong to be married and wrong to eat certain foods. But God created those foods to be eaten with thanks by faithful people who know the truth. Since everything God created is good, we should not reject any of it but receive it with thanks."

The messengers of Satan were the Pharisees who taught the doctrines of demons. This teaching was not about lying, stealing and killing people. It was about abstaining from the free gifts given by God, including marriage and food. They taught that one could become holy by celibacy and fasting. We see similar teaching today in certain forms of Christianity when these preachers will not sell all their possessions by following Christ's commandments, but instead put heavy burdens on their congregations like forbidding jewelry, entertainment and enforcing certain dress codes that seem holy. All these rules and regulations are not from Christ but from the old covenant mindset that was called the "doctrine of demons". This teaching rejects the free gifts of God and tries to attain holiness by self-denial and false humility. Worldliness is not about loving money, sports, music, food, marriage, friends, etc., but it was about the old covenant system of false religion. True religion is to know the love of God and to accept His free gifts. This results in generosity and compassion to those who are weak, instead of trying to impose harsh religious rules on them.

Now although marriage was a free gift from God, the Lord Jesus and Paul warned the Jews not to be consumed by it.

*1st Corinthians 7:26-31 "I think that it is good therefore, **because of the distress that is on us**, that it is good for a man to be as he is. Are you bound to a wife? Don't seek to be freed. Are you free from a wife? **Don't seek a wife**. But if you marry, you have not sinned ... But I say this, brothers: **the time is short**, that from now on, both those who have wives may be as though they had none; and those who weep, as though they didn't weep; and those who rejoice, as though they didn't rejoice; and those who buy, as though they didn't possess; and those who use the world, as not using it to the fullest. **For the mode of this world passes away**."*

Paul told the Jews in Corinth that the time was short because they were living in the time of great distress/tribulation, and therefore he told them to avoid marriage if possible. Those who were already married were not in sin. But if someone could avoid marriage then it would be better, because of the great persecution suffered by the Church where the Jews were killing Christians. Their world was passing away and was soon going to end in 70AD.

Luke 17:28-33 "They ate, they drank, they married, they were given in marriage, until the day that Noah entered into the ship, and the flood came, and destroyed them all. Likewise, even as it was in the days of Lot: they ate, they drank, they bought, they sold, they planted, they built; but in the day that Lot went out from Sodom, it rained fire and sulfur from the sky, and destroyed them all. It will be the same way in the day that the Son of Man is revealed. In that day, he who will be on the housetop, and his goods in the house, let him not go down to take them away.

Let him who is in the field likewise not turn back. Remember Lot's wife! Whoever seeks to save his life loses it, but whoever loses his life preserves it."

Jesus told the Jews not to be choked by the things of life like eating, drinking, buying, selling and getting married because Jerusalem was going to be destroyed in 70AD just like the time of Noah's flood and when Sodom was destroyed by fire. They were told to be busy preaching the Gospel and saving as many Jews as possible before the judgment came upon the Old Covenant system in their generation. They were living in the last days and 2nd coming of Christ. Ever since 70AD, we have enjoyed marriage, eating, drinking and all the free gifts of life for the last 2000 years, thanks to Jesus and His finished work. This world will not end, and God has saved all humanity, therefore let us celebrate and enjoy life.

Unfortunately, there are other burdens found today in religion. They quote this 2nd Corinthians 6:14 telling Christians not to marry people from other religions. But that was only true under the Old Covenant. According to the Law, if the Jews married people from other religions and started worshipping idols, then they would break the Law and bring judgment upon themselves. Paul repeated the same commandment to the Jewish believers in Corinth because the Law had not yet passed away. They were commanded to abstain from worshipping idols, and that is why Paul told them not to be unequally yoked with unbelievers because they were joining their spouses in worshipping idols (2nd Corinthians 6:16). Such rules do not apply anymore because the Law has passed away. **There is no condemnation if you have married a non-Christian**. All of humanity is righteous in Christ because the Law passed away in 70AD and we are not under the Law.

Some of us think that divorce is a sin because God hated divorce in Malachi 2:16. But according to the context, we see that God was warning the Levite Priests in Jerusalem who were breaking the Law by worshipping idols and mistreating the poor. They were also dealing treacherously with their wives by divorcing them. In those days, if a man divorced his wife, then she would be in financial trouble because women did not work. **God hated the way the priests and Jews were abusing and forsaking their wives by throwing them out on the streets by refusing to help them**. God did not hate divorce in general, but He despised their heartless injustice towards the weak. God knows that marriage can be difficult and therefore some people choose to divorce because there is no other option. Let love and common sense take priority over religious rules because there is no condemnation.

The doctrine of demons was the teaching of man's self-righteousness that told people to sacrifice their desires to please God. It is the preaching of Old Covenant teachings to people under the New Covenant. It tells us to tithe 10% of our income so that God will bless us when He does not even need our money, because He is the one who provided us the money in the first place. It tells us to sacrifice our weekends when the truth is that God has given it to enjoy life. It tells us to abstain from secular music when the truth is that God gave man the talents to create all music. It tells us to give up the food that God has prepared and provided for us. It tells us to avoid good clothes and jewelry when the truth is that God loves to see His children well dressed. It tells us to give up our careers for God when the truth is that He Himself has given us the skills and opportunities for our advancement. It tells us to give up our hobbies for God and spend time in Christian activities, but the truth is that God is happy when we are enjoying our hobbies and pleasures. All such doctrines show that we must please God by our sacrifices, and this goes back to the Old Covenant sacrifices, which God never wanted. **The truth is that God is the One who gave up His life for us so that we enjoy abundant life.** Our sacrifices will always try to nullify what Jesus did on the Cross. The truth is that His loving sacrifice is enough and we don't need to add to it. At times, we hear that God has blessed us, so that we give it back to Him, or that we are stewards of His resources. The truth is that He is not a banker who has given us a loan that must be repaid, but He has given us everything freely. He does not own it anymore and does not take back the gifts that He has freely given to us. We are not stewards, but we are His Sons who own the family business. He has given us marriage, family, friends, good food, money, career, music, clothes, jewelry, fashion to enjoy because He is a good Father.

The False Gospel was the Law

Paul had pronounced the curse on those who preached anything apart from his gospel (Galatians 1:8-9). The gospel he preached was the righteousness of faith in Christ, but the Pharisees were using deception to enter the Churches and compel people to get circumcised (Acts 15:1). They said that one had to be saved by keeping the Law of Moses, including the Ten Commandments. The Law was mediated by the angels in the time of Moses. Therefore Paul said that even if an angel appeared to the believers and preached the Law, then they should avoid it. Paul had called the Pharisees as the false apostles of Satan, who preached another Gospel. This false Gospel was the Law.

2nd Corinthians 11:2-4,13-14 "For I am jealous over you with a godly jealousy. For I married you to one husband, that I might present you as a pure virgin to Christ.

*But I am afraid that somehow, as **the serpent deceived Eve** in his craftiness, so your minds might be corrupted from the simplicity that is in Christ. For if **he who comes preaches** another Jesus, whom we did not preach, or if you receive a different spirit, which you did not receive, or **a different "good news"** ... For such men are **false apostles**, deceitful workers, masquerading as Christ's apostles. And no wonder, for even Satan masquerades as an angel of light."*

It was because the Pharisees were deceiving the Church by tempting them to return to their old husband, the Law (Romans 7:1-4). It was just like the serpent had tempted Eve to desire the righteousness through the knowledge of good and evil (Law), instead of the free gift of God (Grace). These Pharisees were the false prophets and workers of iniquity that Christ warned about in Matthew 7:15-23.

*Galatians 3:1-2 "Foolish Galatians, who has **bewitched** you not to obey the truth, before whose eyes Jesus Christ was openly portrayed among you as crucified? I just want to learn this from you. Did you receive the Spirit by the works of the **law**, or by hearing of faith?"*

Paul preached the Gospel of salvation in Christ that would redeem people from the curse and wrath of the Law. So if anyone preached salvation through the Law, then the curse fell upon them. This false gospel brought a curse on the one who preached and the one who believed in the Law. This was because the Law brought a curse on anyone who trusted in it (Galatians 3:10-11). This curse of the Law was fully manifested in 70AD when Jerusalem and the Old Covenant system was destroyed in the fire, thereby fulfilling the curse of Malachi 4:6 upon the land of Israel. This event was the final judgment in the parable of the Sheep and the Goats, when the messengers of Satan were cast into the fire in 70AD.

*Matthew 25 "Then he will say also to those on the left hand, 'Depart from me, you **cursed**, into the eternal fire which is prepared for the devil and his angels"*

At that time, the old order of the Law had passed away, and all things became new (new covenant) (Revelation 21:1-5). The Law and the curses passed away. Today the entire world is under the New Covenant of Grace and therefore there is no more curse (Revelation 22:3). The true Gospel for today is that Jesus has already made us righteous by His grace. We believe this good news to experience the love of the Father and freedom from guilt and fear. There is no more curse today, because the nation of Israel has been restored to their land despite their unbelief in Christ. This proves that nobody can be under any curse even if they preach a Gospel that is not fully accurate.

Satan was defeated and does not exist anymore.

I want to show you something remarkable. You don't need to rebuke Satan and cast out demons because Satan was destroyed in 70AD. The first instance of Satan or the serpent was found in Genesis 3:2 when Eve was tempted to become like God. This serpent was responsible for the system of judging man based on the works of good and evil. Later on, this manifested as the Ten Commandments in the Law of Moses. The word "Satan" means accuser and that is what he is called here:

Revelation 12:10-11 "Now the salvation, and the power, and the kingdom of our God and the authority of His Christ have come, for the accuser of our brethren has been thrown down, he who accuses them before our God day and night. And they overcame him because of the blood of the Lamb and because of the word of their testimony, and they did not love their life even when faced with death."

This "Satan" was accusing the Jewish brethren of Christ, and in John 5:45 it says that the Law of Moses accused the Jews of sin. Therefore the Law and Satan are the same! Now, some will ask why God would give the Law? The Law is holy and perfect in itself, but it kills and condemns. Satan was also known as the liar and deceiver who did not announce that it was coming to kill, steal and destroy. God created all things good but told Adam to stay away from rules. The Law appeared good, but it resulted in death. You see, the Law cannot make anything perfect, but it was given to increase sin (Hebrews 7:19, Romans 5:20). The Law is good, but it was never God's will for man to be under the Law. God had to give man free will, and it was man's choice to be self-righteous under the Law. This "Satan" is nothing but the essence of the flesh – it is man's self-righteousness that accuses other people.

When Peter tried to stop Jesus from going to the cross, the Lord told Satan to get behind Him. It was not because evil spirits possessed Peter, but because he used human wisdom to prevent Jesus from doing the will of God. When Jesus called the Pharisees, the children of the devil, it did not mean that Satan was their father. He meant that they were practicing the same accusation of the Law against others. The Law had the power to kill people spiritually and steal their eternal inheritance. But thanks to Jesus Christ, He overcame the Law on the cross, and the bride of Christ also overcame during the great tribulation. Isn't it amazing that Satan defeated the first Adam and his wife, and this resulted in the condemnation of all people? But now the last Adam, Jesus Christ and His wife (the Church) overcame the Law (Satan) and made all of humanity righteous in the New Covenant!

In Revelation 12:10, it indicated that there was a specific time when Satan would be defeated. It was "now"; at the time John wrote the book of Revelation. When was that time?

*John 12:31-32 "**Now** is the judgment of this world. Now the prince of this world will be cast out. And I, if I am lifted up from the earth, will draw **all** people to myself."*

The judgment and destruction of Satan were fulfilled in the time of Christ, and specifically during the last generation of the old covenant Jews in 70AD, when the Law came to an end. Satan or the ministry of the Ten Commandments (Law) was defeated. At that time, Christ saved all of humanity.

Well if the devil does not exist, then why is there evil in the world? It's not because of any devil, but because of man's wrong thinking. The world is not perfect at all. People are not inherently evil, but they do crazy things. It's not because of a lack of "commandments", but because of many unexpected and unplanned reasons–bad childhood, religious teaching, oppression, misfortune, racism, inequality, poverty, etc.

Now of course, there are many instances of the devil in the Bible, but they mostly point to human influences. The "morning star" of Isaiah 14:12 was referring to the king of Babylon who was destroyed by the Assyrians. When people were demon-possessed in the time of Christ, it was mental sickness caused by the oppressive burdens and guilt from the Law. When Jesus told them that they were forgiven, many of them were healed, and these supposed demons fled from them. This was because they were mental problems and not an imaginary being called "Satan". When Peter spoke about the devil being like a devouring lion, he was talking about the Pharisees who persecuted the believers all over the world.

When Paul spoke of principalities and powers of darkness in Ephesians 6:12, he was talking about the Pharisees and teachers of the Law who crucified Christ and the Church. When Paul spoke of putting on the armor of Christ to withstand the day of evil in Ephesians 6:11, he was telling them to flee from the Old Covenant and trust in Jesus, before the "day of the Lord" that destroyed the Temple in 70AD. The armor of God is not a burdensome suit, but it is Christ Himself (Isaiah 59:16-20). That is why Paul told the Roman Jews to clothe themselves with Christ to avoid being judged in 70AD (Romans 13:10-14). The "god of the world" of 2nd Corinthians 4:4 was nothing but the Ten Commandments and the Law, that put a veil on the eyes of the Jews as Paul described in 2nd Corinthians 3:14.

The rulers and authorities of the world were the Pharisees who crucified Christ (1st Corinthians 2:6). When Jesus destroyed Jerusalem and the Law in 70AD, that was when all authority, power and dominion came under His feet. That was when "Satan" was crushed under the feet of the Church in Romans 16:20. That was the judgment day of the old covenant world. This "Satan", which was also known as the system of judgment based on good and evil, was finally cast into the lake of fire in Jerusalem in 70AD. This was simply the declaration that God destroyed the system of the Law, and Christ has saved the world. Satan, the Law, sin, guilt, spiritual death, judgment and condemnation have passed away.

You cannot lose salvation

Some people go through great religious burdens in trying to please God by faith and avoiding sin, in the fear that they could lose salvation if they do not perform according to the high expectations found in the Bible. This is because of a lack of understanding of the Covenants and what happened in 70AD. **The people of the 1st Century were called out of the Law to put their faith in Christ. If they remained under the Law, then they would lose salvation.** To be under the Law was to be in the flesh and remain in sin, but to trust in Christ was to be in the Spirit and having His righteousness.

Romans 8:12-13 "So then, brothers, we are debtors, not to the flesh, to live after the flesh. For if you live after the flesh, you must die; but if by the Spirit you put to death the deeds of the body, you will live."

All of Paul's epistles were telling the Jews and Greek converts to not go back to the Law. That is what he meant by living in the flesh. If they went back to the law, then they would perish in the judgment of 70AD. This is why he told the Galatians to crucify their "flesh" by not trusting in the Law. To crucify the flesh was to simply trust in Christ and not in the sacrifice of the Law. He told them that if they sowed to the flesh, they would reap destruction (Galatians 6:7). The sowing in the flesh only meant that they were trusting in the circumcision of the flesh.

Galatians 6:12-13 **"As many as desire to look good in the flesh, they compel you to be circumcised**; *only that they may not be persecuted for the cross of Christ. For even they who receive circumcision don't keep the law themselves, but* **they desire to have you circumcised, that they may boast in your flesh"**

He told them that they were in Christ, being in the Spirit (Romans 8:9) and that they were actually circumcised in the Spirit and not by religious works of the Law (Philippians 3:3).

Galatians 5:1-7 "Stand firm therefore in the liberty by which Christ has made us free, and don't be entangled again with a yoke of bondage. Behold, I, Paul, tell you that if you receive circumcision, Christ will profit you nothing. Yes, I testify again to every man who receives circumcision, that he is a debtor to do the whole law. You are alienated from Christ, you who desire to be justified by the law. You have fallen away from grace. For we, through the Spirit, by faith wait for the hope of righteousness. For in Christ Jesus neither circumcision amounts to anything, nor uncircumcision, but faith working through love. You were running well! Who interfered with you that you should not obey the truth?"

They were running the race from out of the Law and into the final destination of salvation in Christ. If they went back to the Law, they would miss out on the prize and Christ would be of no use to them. That is why Paul said that he was running a race and hoping to win the prize (1st Corinthians 9:24-27). He was killing his desire for the Law and instead trusting in Jesus to attain the righteousness by faith. He told them to run the race so that they could receive the prize of salvation. This is why Paul told the Church that they would receive salvation only if they continued in the faith (Colossians 1:22-23). This is why Paul told them to work out their salvation with fear and trembling (Philippians 2:12) because some of them were arguing about circumcision and going back to the Law. **Today we don't have to work out our salvation because we were never under the Law and we are already saved! We are already at the finish line because Christ has won the race for us.**

Acts 20:32 "Now, brothers, I entrust you to God, and to the word of his grace, which is able to build up, and to give you the inheritance among all those who are sanctified"

Paul warned the Ephesians that there would be false teachers that preached the Law to bring divisions and take away their inheritance. So he told them to hold on to the Gospel of Grace that would build them up. But if they went back to the Law and judged one another using the Law, instead of building each other up in grace, then the Spirit would be grieved (Ephesians 4:29-30). Grieving the Spirit was all about going back to the Old Covenant and not applicable to us today because we live in the new covenant where there is no more sin or law.

The Apostle Peter also had several warnings to his Jewish brethren who were going back to the Law. The judgment was falling upon their generation, and that is why he called the believers as the chosen generation and royal priesthood because the unbelieving Jews were the wicked generation and the false priesthood. (1st Peter 2:9, Acts 2:40). He told them that they would be the ones to witness Christ's 2nd coming (1st Peter 1:13, 2nd Peter 1:11). He also told them to stop twisting the words of Paul who also warned the Jews to forsake the Law before Christ's 2nd coming in 70AD (2nd Peter 3:15). Peter described the Jews who went back to the Law like dogs going back to their vomit (2nd Peter 2:22). That was the true definition of backsliding. It has nothing to do with not going to Church or being uninterested in Christian things. Today you cannot backslide or become lukewarm because you were already born righteous in Christ under the new covenant. **We cannot fall away or backslide to the Law when it does not even exist. We are seated in Christ.**

Jesus had many difficult things to say to the Jews in the Gospels and the book of Revelation. He told them that if they denied His name, then He would also deny them at the judgment (Matthew 10:33). But we know that Peter denied Christ three times and was yet graciously chosen as one of the Apostles. Denying the name of Christ was to accept the Law and come under its curse. It was a specific calling to the Jews (Matthew 10:5-6) and is not applicable today. The Law does not exist today, and therefore **God is faithful even if we are unfaithful because we are one with Him and He cannot deny himself** (2nd Timothy 2:13). Christ also told his disciples to sell their possessions and leave behind their jobs and families because Jerusalem was going to be destroyed in 70AD. The true believers obeyed His commandments. But there were some Jews, like Ananias and Sapphira who tried to deceive the Church by not selling all their possessions so that they could take money that was meant for the poor. They died on the spot because of great fear that came when they were caught red-handed. God did not strike them dead, but they died because they were still under the Law that brought guilt and fear. You will never see such things happening today in Churches. **Today we should not use the story of Ananias and Sapphira to extract tithes and donations because Christ has not commanded us to sell our possessions.**

The blasphemy of the Spirit was the unforgivable sin that was committed by the Jews. It was because they rejected the Father for 1500 years, and then they rejected the Son by crucifying Him. They finally rejected the Holy Spirit when they persecuted the Apostles by accusing them of being led by the devil (Law). It was ironic because it was the Pharisees themselves who did the work of Satan (accusation). Their final judgment came in 70AD. Today we live in the New Covenant where God does not account sins anymore. Today even if people say evil things about the Father, Son and Holy Spirit, they are already forgiven. Jesus also gave the Churches in Revelation warnings like being blotted out of **the Book of Life**. This does not apply to us because the book of Revelation was written to the seven churches in

Asia who were living in the last days before the final judgment and resurrection in 70AD. The Book of Life was a Jewish book of the Law. If their names were in this book, then they received salvation from the curse of the Law (Deuteronomy 29:20-21). Only those who crucified Christ were blotted from the book of life (Psalm 69:4,29 & John 15:25). This was specific to the Jews. **Today our names are engraved in the palm of Christ and cannot be blotted out (Isaiah 49:16).**

The book of Jude is one of the smallest books in the Bible, but it is very similar to the Epistle of James. Both of them were written to the Jews under the Law.

*Jude 1:11,14-15,18-22,24 "Woe to them! For they ran riotously in the error of Balaam for hire, and **perished** in Korah's rebellion ... **About these** also Enoch, prophesied, saying, "Behold, **the Lord came** with ten thousands of his holy ones, **to execute judgment** on all ... "In the last time there will be mockers, walking after their own ungodly lusts. "**These are they** who cause divisions, and are sensual, not having the Spirit. **But you**, beloved, keep building up yourselves on your most holy faith ... **looking for the mercy of our Lord Jesus Christ to eternal life**. On some have compassion ... some save, **snatching them out of the fire** ... Now to him who is able to keep them from stumbling, and to **present you faultless before the presence of his glory in great joy"***

Jude spoke about the Pharisees who followed the teaching of Balaam because they were lovers of money and not God. They preached the Law and made money from all the people by taking tithes and donations, but pronounced curses on the poor Jews who trusted in Christ. They persecuted the Church and deceived the Jews by taking them back to the Law. Jude said that the 2nd coming of Christ was going to bring judgment on them because they were living in the "last time". He told the believers to snatch them out of the fire before Jerusalem was destroyed. The believers would be declared faultless at His 2nd coming in 70AD. The judgment is over, and the world is at peace with God.

The book of Hebrews is a book that has brought great fear to many believers. First of all, this book was written to the Jews who were coming out of the Old Covenant and entering the New Covenant of Christ. It was written to the Jews telling them to escape the wrath of the Law that came in 70AD. It was not written to us because we were not born under the Old Covenant. People think that they are crucifying Jesus all over again if they fall into some sin (Hebrews 6:6). They worry that if they are not holy in their behavior, then they would not see the Lord (Hebrews 12:14). They think that if they willfully sin, then there is no more sacrifice left but only God's raging fire of judgment (Hebrews 10:27). The willful sin was only for the Jews to go back to the Law in unbelief, in spite of hearing the Gospel with all its signs and wonders that were performed by Christ and the Apostles. For them to go back to the animal sacrifices of the Law meant that Christ had to be crucified all over again. They had to become holy by trusting in Christ; otherwise, they would not see Him in his 2nd coming. They could not escape the raging fire of judgment that fell upon them in 70AD. It has absolutely nothing to do with us. Today we are already perfect in the New Covenant, without any sin.

There is no more fear in Christ

Chapter 5

Jesus has finished the work

The Christian life is a long journey for many people. It begins with realizing that they are sinners. Then they get baptized by faith in Christ, followed by joining a Church, studying the Bible, attending weekly services, confessing sins, being filled with the Spirit, serving in Church or ministry, trying hard to be a good Christian, enduring trials in the wilderness. The end of the journey is to finally reach heaven if you have been faithful and not given up or fallen into sin. I have experienced all of this, and it was because I did not know the finished work of Christ.

Christ's finished work–Cross, Resurrection, Return

The Christian world unanimously agrees on the Cross and Resurrection of Christ but is divided about the 2nd coming of Christ. This is one of the main reasons why I believe that we are not sure of salvation. It's because we have tried to insert ourselves into the Bible, in the shoes of the 1st Century Christians who were transitioning between the Old and New Covenants. We hear about the finished work of the Cross of Christ, and Paul said that He preached Christ and Him crucified. But can the cross be the finished work by itself? Without the resurrection, the faith would be useless, and people would still be in their sins (1st Corinthians 15:14-17). Christ's resurrection alone would be incomplete unless He returned in His 2nd coming to judge the world. Therefore the finished work of Christ began at the cross, continued in the resurrection and was completed in His 2nd coming in 70AD. The reason the work of Christ is unfinished in the minds of many Christians is that they are not aware of His 2nd and final coming in 70AD.

Therefore millions of Christians are unsure of their destiny and think that their sins may result in losing salvation.

The people in the 1st Century Church were looking forward to the salvation through His 2nd coming.

*Hebrews 9:28 "Christ also, having been offered once to bear the sins of many, will appear a second time, without sin, to those who are **eagerly** waiting for him for salvation."*

This was the salvation from the wrath of the Law that was imminently going to fall upon the Jews and their system of Law through the destruction of Jerusalem in 70AD. All these are clearly mentioned in Romans 4:15, 1st Thessalonians 2:16, Luke 21:20-24, Romans 2:5, Romans 1:18, Revelation 14:10.

Salvation was a three-step process of body, soul and spirit for the Thessalonians, Corinthians, Philippians, Romans, Galatians and all the people under the old covenant. They were waiting till the Lord's 2nd coming to be declared blameless in body, soul and spirit (1st Thessalonians 5:23). They were waiting for the resurrection to receive the righteousness of faith (Galatians 5:5, Romans 8:11,19, Philippians 3: 20-21). The 1st Century Church had to go through the process of sanctification in their life on earth. When they died, their spirits would be separated in hades till His 2nd coming. At Christ's 2nd coming, they were resurrected to receive their salvation when Christ ended the Law and the Temple in 70AD.

So now today we are already born in that salvation because we are not in the Old Covenant, but in the New Covenant where there is no more sin. Our body, soul and spirit are completely perfect because we are born holy. We are already sanctified because Christ Himself is our sanctification.

*1st Corinthians 1:30 "Because of him, **you are in Christ Jesus, who was made to us wisdom from God, and righteousness and sanctification, and redemption**"*

Our spirits are already perfect and righteous because we were born in the New Jerusalem (Hebrews 12:20-23).

We have everlasting righteousness, and we cannot become sinners anymore

The Apostle Paul was living in the last generation under the Law. They were all sinners under the Old Covenant and were waiting for the Messiah to save them from the wrath of the Law. They were waiting eagerly for the righteousness that was by faith in Christ.

Galatians 5:5 "For we, through the Spirit, by faith wait for the hope of righteousness"

Philippians 3:8-9 "that I may gain Christ and be found in him, not having a righteousness of my own, that which is of the law, but that which is through faith in Christ, the righteousness which is from God by faith."

They were waiting for Jesus Christ to come and bring His righteousness by destroying the enemies who were the Old Covenant ministers in their Temple in 70AD.

Isaiah 59:17-21 NLT "He put on righteousness as his body armor and placed the helmet of salvation on his head ... He will repay his enemies for their evil deeds ... The Redeemer will come to Jerusalem to buy back those in Israel who have turned from their sins," says the LORD ... And this is my covenant I will make with them."

Christ saved all Israel who finally turned away from the sin of trusting in the Law (Romans 11:26-27) At that time the entire world was made righteous because the Law was taken away and God made a New Covenant.

But before that time, if anyone went back to the Law and trusted in their works, then they would become sinners.

Galatians 2:16-19 "by the works of the law no one will be justified. "But if, in seeking to be justified in Christ, we Jews find ourselves also among the sinners, doesn't that mean that Christ promotes sin? Absolutely not! If I rebuild what I destroyed, then I really would be a lawbreaker. For I through the law, died to the law."

If they returned to the dead system of the Law, then they would be judged as law-breakers, because nobody could become righteous by the Law. They were setting aside the grace of God, and Christ's death meant nothing to them. Today we cannot become sinners anymore because the Law that imputed sin has finally passed away in 70AD. Where there is no Law, there is no sin (Romans 4:15).

We are perfect in Christ

Most Christians celebrate the birth of Christ at Christmas. We commemorate the death of Christ on Good Friday. We celebrate the resurrection at Easter. But very few know that His 2nd coming has already happened. This is the biggest problem today because we do not realize our position and identity in Christ. We are still trying to have Christ born in our hearts when it already happened 2000 years ago. We are still trying to carry a cross that was never commanded to us. We are trying to attain to the righteousness of faith and the resurrection, without knowing that it already came in 70AD. Now here is the missing link. Today our position with Christ is not in the virgin birth or the cross or even the resurrection. We are seated with Christ in the heavenly places according to Ephesians 2:6. Now, what does it mean to be seated with Christ? What exactly happened when Christ sat down at the right hand of the Father?

Hebrews 1:3 NIV "After he had provided purification for sins, he sat down at the right hand of the Majesty in heaven."

It says that Christ sat down AFTER He provided the purification of all sins committed by those under the Law.

*Hebrews 10:10-14 "**we have been sanctified through the offering of the body of Jesus Christ once for all**. Every priest indeed stands day by day serving and often offering the same sacrifices, which can never take away sins, but **he, when he had offered one sacrifice for sins forever, sat down on the right hand of God**; from that time waiting until his enemies are made the footstool of his feet. For by one offering he has **perfected forever**"*

Under the Law, the high priest had to repeatedly offer sacrifices that could never take away sin. This is because it was an imperfect sacrifice of animals offered by an imperfect priest in a man-made Temple that was destroyed in 70AD. But when Christ came, He was the perfect priest who never sinned, and He offered the perfect sacrifice and entered the presence of the Father in heaven. After He had done this, He sat down, because the work was finished. He perfected the human race, and therefore He sat down because there was no more sacrifice for sin. He could not make us anymore righteous than Himself! Jesus took away the sacrifice of the Law by taking away sins forever, and He made us perfect forever. He was then waiting for the enemies (Pharisees) to be crushed under His feet.

Paul wrote in Romans 16:20 that the enemies were crushed under the feet of the Church, which is the body of Christ in 70AD. That was when the Law was completely eradicated, and all of humanity was made perfect. For the last 1946 years, since 70AD, all of humanity has been permanently seated with Christ, having been made perfect without any sin.

This is what Jesus says to you and me.

Song of Songs 4:7 NIV "You are altogether beautiful, my darling; **there is no flaw in you.***"*

Colossians 2:9-10 NIV "For in Christ all the fullness of the Deity lives in bodily form, and **in Christ you have been brought to fullness.***"*

There is no flaw in you and me because we have been brought to perfection and completion in Christ. Just as Christ has the fullness of God in Him, we also have God's perfection and righteousness. There is no room for improvement in us.

Ephesians 2:8 "you have been saved....For we are his workmanship, created in Christ Jesus for good works, which God prepared before that we would walk in them."

You were saved and made alive almost 2000 years ago when Jesus finished the work. We are God's masterpiece and workmanship created in Christ. Don't you know that everything God made is good and perfect? God ordained all our works in this world, even before time began. We don't do good works so that we grow closer to God or become perfect or more spiritual, but everything has already been preplanned because we are already perfect in Christ. God made you perfect in Himself.

Following Jesus or Resting in His work?

So now that we are perfect, do we have to follow Jesus and do all the things He did? Let me answer this with the story of Adam. When God created Adam, he was perfect in righteousness, and he did not know he was naked. It was the law that told him he was naked. Adam had to be clothed with Christ and His righteousness because He took away the Law. So now people are born, clothed in Christ already. We were never in sin or born in sin because we were always in Christ. But the big problem is that religion tells them that they are naked and that they are sinners who need to do something by faith and works to become clothed. Do you see what is going on? We have changed Christ's completed work into an unfinished work. The true Gospel is to remind ourselves that we are already clothed and alive in Christ.

Adam did not have to do anything to become like God because He was already created in God's image. **In the same way, we have nothing to do to become like Christ anymore. We are already fully mature in Christ.** We don't need to ask Christ to be born into our hearts every Christmas. We don't need to fast as He did for 40 days during Lent. We don't need to carry the cross to become like Him. We don't need to attain the resurrection. The people in the Bible had to follow Christ in the wilderness because they had not yet received their salvation. We cannot follow Jesus because He already lives in us. You cannot become something that you already have. The people in the Bible were told to press on to perfection and be holy as Christ because they were under the Law. But today we are already as perfect and holy as Christ is in the New Covenant.

Colossians 2:6,8 "As therefore you received Christ Jesus, the Lord, walk in him ... Be careful that you don't let anyone rob you through his philosophy and vain deceit, after the tradition of men"

If religion tells you to tithe or get baptized or fast or do anything because Jesus commanded it, then ask them whether they are following Jesus by selling all their possessions and giving it to the poor? Are they picking up their cross, hating their lives, forsaking their families and leaving everything to become His disciples? I am 100% sure that they are not obeying Jesus. Do you know why? It's because Jesus did not command any of those things to us today. It was for the people under the Old Covenant before the Judgment of 70AD when the Law passed away. Today we are in the New Covenant, where God made a New Way–no more commandments and therefore, there is no more sin. He made all of humanity perfect in Christ's finished work. Now if you want to get baptized, fast, tithe and do all the Christian activities, then you are free to do so. But it does not make you more pleasing to God, and it does not make you more righteous. Even if you do absolutely nothing, He has already done the work.

The fruit of the Spirit manifests when people stop trusting in their efforts. When they stop trusting in their performance of loving others or trying to keep the Ten Commandments or trying to be a good person, then the Spirit within them bears the fruit of love, joy, peace, etc. This happens when you are not under pressure or expectation to fulfill any laws. This is why it is effortless, and it is God working within you. I now understand why the most compassionate people are the ones who don't know the Bible or are not very involved in Church. It's because they don't keep track of their good deeds, but effortlessly flow with the love that is already within them.

No more curse – It is DONE

The curse started when Adam sinned. But before this happened, we see that God told Adam just to enjoy all the free gifts that were created. God told him to stay away from knowing about good and evil because it would kill him. It was religion and laws that brought the curse on humanity, and that manifested as the Law of Moses and the Ten Commandments. God never wanted man to be under religion. God is selfless and does not want man to relate to Him through knowing good and evil. He only wanted to create everything and give it to us to enjoy life without religious rules, so that we know His love for us.

When the Jews desired to be under the Law, they put themselves under the curse, because the Law demanded perfect obedience.

Galatians 3:10 "For as many as are of the works of the law are under a curse. For it is written, "Cursed is everyone who doesn't continue in all things that are written in the book of the law, to do them."

Everyone who even attempted to keep the Law was under the curse. Jesus Christ died on the cross to become the curse of Israel so that all who believed in Him would receive blessings instead of curses. So then, in that last generation of Israel between 30-70AD, the Jews were called to put their faith to escape the curse of the Law. Otherwise their land would be destroyed by the curse (Malachi 4:6). There was no lower point for the Jews than seeing the pagan Roman armies destroy their nation and Temple. It was surely the self-appointed curse upon the people of Israel because they ignored the repeated and heartfelt cry of Jesus to escape such a horrible judgment.

Luke 19:41-44 NLT "But as he came closer to Jerusalem and saw the city ahead, he began to weep. "How I wish today that you of all people would understand the way to peace. But now it is too late, and peace is hidden from your eyes. Before long your enemies will build ramparts against your walls and encircle you and close in on you from every side. They will crush you into the ground, and your children with you. Your enemies will not leave a single stone in place, because you did not recognize it when God visited you."

The Jews did not recognize God who visited them in Christ's first coming, and therefore the curse fell upon the land in 70AD, to fulfill all things at that time (Luke 21:20-22). At that time, God finally removed the old covenant system and its curse from the face of the earth and made these two stunning declarations.

Revelation 22:3 "THERE WILL BE NO CURSE ANY MORE"

When Adam sinned, he had invited the curse upon the land so that he would not enjoy the fruit of his labor (Genesis 3:17). This was fulfilled in 70AD, because the Jews who worked to attain salvation by keeping the Law, actually received the curse of the land when Jerusalem was destroyed. We also know that the believing Jews escaped the curse of Adam, because Christ took the curse on the cross, especially when He sweat drops of blood on the land, thereby removing the curse (Luke 22:44). That was how the curse of Adam was lifted from all humanity.

At that time all the curses of the Law of Moses in Deuteronomy 28, also came to an end. All generational curses also came to an end. Today we cannot come under any curse because there is no Law, and therefore no sin. Jesus Christ defeated the curses of Adam and the Law of Moses. We are not born in Adam, nor are we fighting with the flesh or the Law anymore. The race of Adam has passed away, and Christ has created a new humanity where there is no more Jew or Gentile. There are no more sinners, but only righteous sons of God. The ultimate curse of the Law was separation from God in heaven, and Christ removed that curse so that now God's presence is with us both in this life and forever. The battle is over, and Christ has won the victory. Today we are not living in parallel covenants where the believer is under the New Covenant, and the unbeliever is in the Old Covenant. Not a single human being is under the curse. The Old Covenant has passed away, and all of humanity is under the New Covenant.

Today even if your job is a struggle, it's not because of any curse, but it's because life is not perfect in this world. The curse of Adam is gone, and you are God's beloved son. Whether you have a good job or a bad job or are unemployed, there is no curse on you. God is with you always, and His love will never end for you. The curse of Eve is also gone. Some people misunderstood the curse upon Eve, by saying that women will be saved only through childbirth and that those who cannot have children are cursed. But the truth is that verse in 1st Timothy 2:15 was talking about the descendant of Eve, who was Jesus Christ who was born under the Law to take away the curse from all women irrespective of whether they have children or not. Even if a woman cannot have children, she is blessed because Christ descended from Eve and removed the curse.

The curse was the separation of man from God through the Law, but now in the New Covenant, God dwells with us in spirit. Yes, we see God blessing both believers and unbelievers with prosperity and long lives. We see people living long and happy lives and yet they don't even go to Church. We also see faithful Christians dying early. This is because physical death and problems in this life are not a curse from God. This world is imperfect, but not under the curse. In Isaiah 65:20, it said that anyone who died under the age of 100 years, was under the curse. This was symbolic language that spoke about Jerusalem after it was restored following the exile in Babylon. The Jews were still under the Law at that time, and the curse was still in effect. That verse does not apply to us anymore.

When people like Freddie Mercury, George Michael, Michael Jackson and John Lennon died, some in the Church thought they were going to hell. But God loves them all, and there is no curse. We see a gay man dying early through some disease or misfortune and think there is a curse. But when the same thing happens to a Christian, then we say that he was suffering for Christ. Such thinking is based on the Old Covenant Law and not based on the Father's heart of love for all humanity. God sees no difference between the faithful Christian, the unbelieving atheist or gay person. Everyone experiences both good and bad in this world. There is no curse on anyone because Christ consumed every curse on the cross so that we have every spiritual blessing in Him before we were even born (Ephesians 1:3).

Revelation 21:5-6 **"Behold I make ALL things NEW.**

IT IS DONE. I am the Alpha and Omega"

The old order of things was everything in the Bible about sin, law, wrath and judgment. Those things have passed away after Jesus began the work on the Cross and finished it in 70AD. The Law was taken away, and the payment for sins is over, and therefore sin has been taken away. The judgment and wrath are over for all those who trusted in the Law. There is no more punishment or curse, but only blessings. The resurrection and reward for good behavior are also over. Today we live in the New Covenant, where there is no more tree of knowing good and evil that kills people spiritually. But today, we only have the tree of life, and we can know God as the Father who loves us unconditionally in this life. At that day in 70AD, salvation came to the world. God made all things new, and He has saved the entire world. **He is the Alpha (First) and Omega (Last) because there is no human being outside His love and grace.** It is why God said that it is done. He did not say that He is doing it now, or that He will do it in the future. It was not an imperfect or unfinished work. He has done it in the past! He has made you righteous and perfect in Christ. There is nothing any human being can "undo" or "do" by their faith or works. Salvation is not a journey or something that we will only attain after death. Jesus has already done everything.

Let the whole world praise Him–our Loving Father and Wonderful Savior–Jesus Christ.

Jesus Christ has finished the work – IT IS DONE

Chapter 6

Faith of Christ

A few years ago, a pastor told me that I had the calling of Abraham and that I had to attain the promises of God without wavering in faith. I was so excited, and I faithfully believed God. But the more I was focused on my faith and how not to waver, the harder it got. After three years of trying hard to believe, I came to a point where I gave up on my efforts and realized that Christ was my faith. It was His faith that had already pleased God and guaranteed His promises for me.

Man's journey of faith from Adam to Christ

Hebrews 11 is the chapter in the Bible that is called the "Hall of Faith" because it talks about the all the great people of faith in the Old Testament. The interesting thing is that God never required faith from Adam because they were "father and son" with a relationship of love. Adam did not need faith because sons don't please their fathers by faith but have a relationship based on the father's love. Faith was required from mankind only after Adam sinned and plunged all of humanity into sin. After Adam's sin, the gift of righteousness and salvation was only given by faith. The first man to have faith was Abel, whose sacrifice pointed to the final sacrifice of Christ.

Hebrews 11:4 "By faith, Abel offered to God a more excellent sacrifice than Cain"

This journey of faith continued throughout God's chosen people from Noah, Abraham & Isaac and all the way to Israel and the 12 tribes. When we talk about the modern day Christian faith today, it consists of believing in Jesus, raising your hand, going to an altar, getting baptized, going to Church, praying, tithing, witnessing, etc. But what was the Biblical faith?

Hebrews 11:33-38 "through faith subdued kingdoms, worked out righteousness, obtained promises, stopped the mouths of lions, quenched the power of fire, escaped the edge of the sword, from weakness were made strong, grew mighty in war, and caused foreign armies to flee. Women received their dead by resurrection. Others were tortured, not accepting their deliverance, that they might obtain a better resurrection. Others were tried by mocking and scourging, yes, moreover by bonds and imprisonment. They were stoned. They were sawn apart. They were tempted. They were slain with the sword. They went around in sheep skins and in goat skins; being destitute, afflicted, ill-treated (of whom the world was not worthy), wandering in deserts, mountains, caves, and the holes of the earth."

I don't know about you, but my small faith is nothing compared to the faith of the people in the Bible. The faith of the Bible was about people who gave up their own lives. Abraham, who had waited for 100 years to have his only son Isaac, gave him up in faith. Rahab, the prostitute, put her life in danger by hiding the Jewish spies in her hometown of Jericho. This faith was supernatural, and it was not by human effort. **It was actually the faith OF Christ Himself**.

Hebrews 12:2-3 "looking to Jesus, the author and perfecter of faith, who for the joy that was set before him endured the cross, despising its shame, and has sat down at the right hand of the throne of God"

The author and finisher of the Biblical faith is Jesus Christ Himself. This "faith" is not of human origin, but it is from God Himself. That is why in Ephesians 2:8, it says that we are saved by grace through faith and that even the faith is a gift. In fact, everything is a gift in Christ – both the grace and the faith. Jesus himself is the gift of God (Romans 5:15).

This faith began in the Old Testament and was finally revealed in Christ. When Christ came, THE FAITH came. Faith was not about our efforts, but it was Christ Himself.

*Galatians 3:24-26 NIV "So the law was our guardian until **Christ came** that we might be justified by faith. Now that **this faith has come**, we are no longer under a guardian. So in Christ Jesus you are all children of God through faith."*

It was the Faith and efforts OF Christ that made us all righteous. He came and displayed the true Biblical faith to save the world.

*Galatians 3:22 KJV "by faith **OF** Jesus Christ"*
*Galatians 2:20 KJV "I live by the faith **OF** the Son of God"*

It was the faith of God that actually created all things!

*Hebrews 11:3 "**By faith**, we understand that the universe has been framed **by the word of God**"*

This faith was the word of God, and the Word is Christ Himself (John 1:1). The word of faith in Romans 10:17 is Christ Himself. When the Bible says that the righteous shall live by faith, it was talking about Christ who is the righteousness of God. This faith was Christ Himself. He created all men and reconciled them all by His faith. The entire world was saved by Christ's faith.

*Colossians 1:16,20 "For **by him** (Christ) all things were created, in the heavens and on the earth .... And through him to **reconcile all** things"*

We are saved by Christ's faith and love

Therefore now we know why Jesus told his disciples to sell all their possessions, give up their jobs, forsake their Jewish religion, leave their families, preach the Gospel and carry the cross of persecution and death. It was because this is what Jesus Himself did in His life and death on the Cross. It was Christ's faith that accomplished all these things. We are not called to do any of those things that Jesus commanded to the Jewish disciples because He finished the work. They had to endure till the end to be saved in 70AD and be raised from the dead, just like Jesus carried the Cross and overcame death. They had to overcome the Law and the Pharisees just like Jesus overcame on the Cross. The Bride of Christ was the 1st century Church, who overcame the Pharisees and the Law by the faith of Christ.

We are not called to do any of those things because Jesus did all of that for us. We don't live under the Law, so now there is nothing for us to overcome or endure. We are not living in the world under the devil (ministry of law) that passed away in 70AD. We live in God's kingdom where Christ reigns in spirit, and all of humanity is righteous. We are already righteous in Christ, and therefore we don't have to attain it by our faith anymore. **The Biblical faith was only required in the Old Creation from the time of Adam till 70AD.** They were called to be righteous by faith because they were born as sinners under the Law. But we have been born in the New Covenant where there is no more sin because Jesus removed the Law. We are not called to follow Jesus to the cross but rest in the fact that He has done everything. We don't have any spiritual or physical cross to carry. We cannot follow Jesus because we are already ONE with Him. You cannot follow someone who already lives in you. He lives in us, and His faith has made us righteous apart from our faith. **We are saved by Christ's perfect faith and works and not by our imperfect faith or devotion.**

Jesus did everything for us. He was born under the Law so that we were born under Grace. He was baptized for us to make the entire world born again through His resurrection. He fasted 40 days without food or water so that we can enjoy and feast in this life and forever. He prayed fervently for us so that we can enjoy the blessings as the children of God. He endured till the end, by being faithful unto death on the cross. He rose from the dead to make us alive and He seated us with Himself in heavenly places as children of God. In 70AD, Jesus finally removed the law, so that God does not give us laws but lavishes His love on us. There is absolutely nothing for us to do. **It was done completely by the faith and work of Jesus Christ so that we are not proud of our faith, but we boast in Christ's faith alone**. The Biblical faith has come through Jesus Christ, and it has made the entire world righteous.

The faith of Abraham was about Jesus

We are told to keep believing and enduring in faith like Abraham. We are told to be like Moses and leave the riches of Egypt, or be like Daniel and others. We are told to have great faith like Abraham and give up our desires and plans, so that we can go where God is telling us to, and give up our Isaac on the altar. All this sounds very spiritual, but it was not meant for us. The true faith of Abraham was all about what Jesus did.

Romans 4:18-25 NIV "Against all hope, Abraham in hope believed ... Without weakening in his faith .... he did not waver through unbelief regarding the promise of God, but was strengthened in his faith and gave glory to God, being fully persuaded that God had power to do what he had promised. This is why "it was credited to him as righteousness."

We know that God made Abraham righteous when he first heard and believed God's promise of having descendants. But this was many years before Isaac was born. He went through a lot of unbelief and even decided to have a son through his maid, Hagar. After many years, he finally received Isaac. But now it says that Abraham endured and believed that God would raise the dead. The Bible tells us when exactly this happened.

Hebrews 11:17-19 "By faith, Abraham, being tested, offered up Isaac. Yes, he who had gladly received the promises was offering up his one and only son; even he to whom it was said, "your offspring will be accounted as from Isaac"; concluding that God is able to raise up even from the dead. Figuratively speaking, he also did receive him back from the dead."

Abraham's endurance in faith was severely tested when God told him to give up Isaac. We can only imagine the great anguish he suffered, when he had to give up his only son, after waiting for more than 100 years to enjoy him. Abraham believed that God would resurrect Isaac even after being sacrificed in death. This act of faith confirmed his righteousness. Now does that mean God is asking us to give up our family lives, careers and desires to become righteous? No, the faith of Abraham was actually fulfilled in what Jesus did. Our Lord Jesus also prayed and endured in faith when He was going to the cross, believing that God would raise Him from the dead.

Hebrews 5:7 "He, in the days of his flesh, having offered up prayers and petitions with strong crying and tears to him who was able to save him from death"

The reason Jesus was raised from the dead was to make us righteous. He was raised FOR our justification.

Romans 4:25 "He was delivered over to death for our sins and was raised to life for our justification."

It was Christ's faith in His own resurrection that made us all righteous. We were raised along with Christ, with no choice of ours. This happened 2000 years ago, and that is why God calls this the gift of His grace. It was His faith that saved us by grace!

Ephesians 2:6,8 "made us alive together with Christ (by grace you have been saved) and raised us up with him, and made us to sit with him in the heavenly places in Christ Jesus...For it is by grace you have been saved, through faith – and this is not from yourselves, it is the gift of God"

So we can declare that Jesus did everything. It was His faith and His grace that saved us – He is both the faith and the grace. All the works that we perform have been preordained before the world began because Jesus already did it for us 2000 years ago. Hallelujah, what a complete and perfect salvation has been given to us apart from our faith or efforts! This is how Jesus Himself is the final fulfillment of the faith of all men under the Old Creation, from Abel, Noah, Abraham, etc. The faith of Abraham was actually fulfilled. We are not called to follow the faith of Abraham, Moses or Daniel or anyone in the Bible because Christ Himself is our faith that raised us up and made us righteous.

Christ's death on the cross also fulfilled His commandment to the Jews to give up their lives and their families to follow Him. (Luke 14:25) When Abraham gave up Isaac, it was a foretaste of how God the Father gave up His family (Christ). Christ gave up His career and family so that we can enjoy our family and career as the free gifts that God has given us. He denied Himself and carried the cross so that we can enjoy ourselves.

Epistle of James – The Faith that required works

The book of James used to be one of my favorite Bible books when I was very confident of my faith and works. I used to love to read the warnings from James because I was very strong in faith. But later on, I understood the truth about this epistle. It was not written to us, but to the 12 tribes of Israel (James 1:1). The Jews were under the Law and were not even saved yet, while James wrote this to them (James 1:21).

The book of James has many warnings. He told the Jews that not many of them should teach because the teachers would be judged severely in the fire (James 3:1-6). But this was not talking about us, but about the teachers of the Law. Today we are qualified in the New Covenant because God made us competent in His grace and not our goodness (2nd Corinthians 3: 5-6). But for the Jews under law, they would perish in the curse of Gehenna (hell) in 70AD, if they cursed others under the Law. This was similar to what Christ told the Jews because they would be judged for every idle word (Matthew 12:36). This was not written to us because we are not under the Law. James called the Jews as enemies of God and adulterers (James 4:4). It was not talking about anyone today because they were the adulterers who cheated on Christ, by going back to the Law who was their old husband (Romans 7:1-5). We are the beloved of Christ and cannot go back to the Law. He told them to resist the devil (Pharisees) and submit to God by following Jesus (James 4:7). Today the devil does not exist, and we have no fear of demons or such things. If the Jews remained in the Law, then they would be sinners. This is why he told them to mourn and come near to God by coming out of the Law (James 4:7-8). Today, we are already near to God, even so much that He lives in our bodies. We cannot get any closer to Him. But the Jews living before 70AD were going back to the Law and thinking that everything would be fine. Therefore James had to drastically warn them to persevere in their faith. **It was not written to us because we are not under the Law and Christ lives in us.**

James 1:12 NIV "Blessed is the one who perseveres under trial because, having stood the test, that person will receive the crown of life that the Lord has promised to those who love him."

They were coming out of the Old Covenant by faith but were undergoing trials through persecution during the great tribulation, so that they could receive the crown of life at Christ's 2nd coming, which was imminent in their lifetime (James 5:8-9).

*1st Peter 4:12-13,17 "Beloved, don't be astonished at the fiery trial which has come upon you, to test you, as though a strange thing happened to you. But because you are partakers of Christ's sufferings, rejoice; that **at the revelation of his glory** you also may rejoice with exceeding joy ... For the **time has come** for judgment to begin with the household of God"*

Peter confirmed that the Jews were suffering with Christ so that they would receive the glory at the resurrection and judgment that was imminent in 70AD. In Hebrews 12:3-11, it says that God disciplined His Jewish children through persecution so that they would be perfected in the faith of Christ. Today, your Father is not testing your faith or disciplining you with persecution and sufferings, because you are His son in Christ who has already perfected you by His faith. He wears the crown and has made you a king, seated with Him in heavenly places, as sons of God. He is your very life because we were made alive with Christ. **All the trials of faith ended in 70AD** when the Law passed away, and all of humanity was made righteous in Christ.

Now, whenever I talk about God's grace without the requirement of works, the common reply is that **faith without works is dead** (James 2:26). It seems that James contradicted what Paul wrote in Romans 4:4-5. But the truth is that scripture does not contradict each other. Both James and Paul were talking to the Jews who were living between 30-70AD. Paul told them not to trust in the Law of Moses, but he also told them to continue in the faith and love, thereby fulfilling the law (Romans 13:8-10). Paul told them not to go back to the Law; otherwise, they would lose their salvation by unbelief. Their "work" was to trust in Jesus and leave the Old Covenant, otherwise, they would be judged by the Law. Christ told the Jews to forsake their 1500-year old traditions from the Old Covenant and leave Jerusalem by believing in Him. This was similar to the "work", that Lot did in leaving Sodom to escape the fire. The "work" that Noah did in faith was to build the ark to escape the flood. The "work" that Rahab did was to save the spies by putting her life in danger. Abraham gave up Isaac by faith, to receive the righteousness that was promised to him when he first believed many years before. In the same way, the Jewish believers received the righteousness, only after enduring the tribulation and finally leaving Jerusalem in 70AD. At that time of Christ's 2nd coming and resurrection, they received the crown of life and the salvation. The unbelieving Jews, who did not persist in faith, remained in Jerusalem, which was destroyed in 70AD. Their "faith" was dead, and it had no works. They trusted in the law and perished. **The Epistle of James was telling the Jews to complete their faith by leaving the old covenant, and it was not written to us. Our faith is complete because Christ did all the work for us by His faith.** The work is finished, and we have Christ's righteousness because His faith attained it for us.

What about being born again through our faith?

If Jesus has already saved us by his faith, then what about being born again by confessing His name? The Christian gospel says that all people in the world are born in sin and therefore need to be born again, by faith in Christ to go to heaven based on the scriptures in John 3:16 and Romans 10:9.

John 3:16, is one of the most famous verses in the Bible which promises eternal life to those who believe in Jesus. In that chapter, Jesus gave the need to be born again to see the kingdom of God. But was this really meant for us today? Let's find out.

*John 3:7-10,14-16 "Don't marvel that I said to you, 'You must be born anew.' The wind blows where it wants to, and you hear its sound, but don't know where it comes from and where it is going. So is everyone who is born of the Spirit." Nicodemus answered him, "How can these things be?" Jesus answered him, "Are you the teacher of **Israel**, and don't understand these things? As Moses lifted up the serpent in the wilderness, even so must the Son of Man be lifted up, **that whoever believes in him should not perish, but have eternal life**. For God so loved the world, that he gave his one and only Son, that whoever believes in him should not perish, but have eternal life."*

Jesus was speaking to Nicodemus, the teacher of the Law of Israel. Jesus said that Israel and all under the old covenant were under the flesh and that they needed to be born of the Spirit. Just like Moses lifted up the bronze serpent in the wilderness and some Israelites were saved from the deadly wound, in the same way, Jesus would be lifted up through His death and resurrection thereby saving the Jews from perishing in the fire of 70AD. How do we know that Jesus was talking about this event?

Luke 13:1-3 "Now there were some present at the same time who told him about the Galileans, whose blood Pilate had mixed with their sacrifices. Jesus answered *them, "Do you think that these Galileans were worse sinners than all the other Galileans, because they suffered such things? I tell you, no, but unless you repent, you will all perish in the **same way**."*

There were some Jews who had rebelled against the Romans and were mercilessly killed by Pilate. Jesus told His disciples that unless they repented, they would also perish in the same manner. The Jews thought that God was going to give them the kingdom through the Old Covenant in Jerusalem and therefore they believed that they were fulfilling the will of God, by fighting against the Romans. But Jesus told the disciples that the kingdom was no longer in Jerusalem, but it was the Holy Spirit dwelling in them. He told them to repent (change their minds) by forsaking the Law and leaving Jerusalem before it was destroyed. He was telling them to forsake the old covenant, Jerusalem and their Temple because God was making a new covenant to include all nations through Jesus Christ. If they believed in Christ, then they would receive salvation from the wrath that fell upon the Jews in 70AD (John 3:36, 1st Thessalonians 2:16)

This is exactly what Paul told the Jews who were trusting in the Law for righteousness and salvation.

*Romans 10:1-6,9,13 "Brothers, my heart's desire and my prayer to God is **for Israel, that they may be saved**.... For being ignorant of God's righteousness, and seeking to establish their own righteousness, they didn't subject themselves to the righteousness of God. **For Christ is the fulfillment of the law for righteousness to everyone** who believes. For Moses writes about the righteousness of the law, "The one who does them will live by them." But the righteousness which is of faith says this ...... that if you will confess with your mouth that Jesus is Lord, and believe in your heart that God raised him from the dead, you will be saved ....**Whoever will call on the name of the Lord will be saved**"*

Paul told them to stop trusting in the Law but to believe in Jesus to be saved. This was because the wrath was the natural consequence, upon those who trusted in the Law (Romans 4:15). They had to believe and confess Jesus as Lord to come out of the Law. The Romans were going to destroy Jerusalem and all the remnants of the Jewish religion throughout the world. Therefore Paul preached the Gospel to the Jew and the Gentile converts, telling them to escape the wrath of the Law (Romans 5:9). Paul told the Jews that whoever called upon the name of Jesus would be saved. These were the same words quoted by Peter, when he preached to the Jews on the day of Pentecost in Acts 2:21. Both Paul and Peter were quoting from the book of Joel, which talked about the destruction of the Old Covenant system of Jerusalem.

Joel 2:31-32 NIV "The sun will be turned to darkness and the moon to blood before the coming of the great and dreadful day of the LORD. And everyone who calls on the name of the LORD will be saved;

for on Mount Zion and in Jerusalem there will be deliverance, as the LORD has said, even among the survivors whom the LORD calls."

Salvation was not found in the old covenant Law of Moses in the earthly Jerusalem because it was going to be destroyed. Salvation and righteousness was given to those in Zion that was the Heavenly Jerusalem through faith in Christ.

Hebrews 12:18,22 "For you have not come to a mountain that might be touched, and that burned with fire.... But you have come to Mount Zion, and to the city of the living God, the heavenly Jerusalem"

The old Jerusalem and the old covenant were destroyed with fire. But the New Jerusalem from heaven offered salvation in the new covenant. This salvation came at the time of resurrection in 70AD, and this was the great hope of Israel.

Acts 23:6 "Men and brothers, I am a Pharisee, a son of Pharisees. Concerning the hope and resurrection of the dead I am being judged!"

When Jesus told Nicodemus to be born again, He was talking about Israel being born again through the resurrection of Christ. Just as all men were dead in Adam, they would be made alive by the resurrection of Christ.

*1st Peter 1:13 "Blessed be the God and Father of our Lord Jesus Christ, who according to his great mercy became our father again to a living hope **through the resurrection** of Jesus Christ from the dead"*

When Jesus rose from the dead, they were made alive with Him and seated with Him in heavenly places (Ephesians 2:1-8). But this was fulfilled in 70AD when they were saved from the wrath and joined Christ in the resurrection of the dead. At that time, they were born again in the Spirit and were one with the Lord.

Galatians 4:5 "He might redeem those who were under the law, that we might receive the adoption of children."

Christ was born under the Law, to give life to the Jews who were waiting to be born again, out from the Old Covenant (Romans 7:23-25). They needed faith to escape the Law, to become born again. They became sons of God, through the resurrection (Romans 8:11-17). Israel was born again through the resurrection at the destruction of the Temple in 70AD.

Isaiah 66:6,8 "A voice of tumult from the city, a voice from the temple, a voice of God that repays what His enemies deserve ... For as soon as Zion travailed, she gave birth to her children"

At that time, the old covenant Israel of the flesh passed away and the new covenant Israel of the spirit, was born again. A new humanity was created, where all of us are in Christ, made righteous and perfect by His faith. Therefore we don't need to believe in Jesus to be saved from a wrath that has already finished in 70AD. Faith was only required from the time of Adam till 70AD because they were under the Law that imputed sin. That Biblical faith was manifested when people gave up their lives, families and possessions, to die as martyrs. We are not called to do any of that because Jesus did it for us. This is why I don't tell anyone to have such a faith because it was not commanded to us. Today we only need to know the good news, that Jesus has already saved us by removing the Law. This will give us peace and joy, knowing that we don't have to depend on our imperfect faith. We don't need to be born again or become righteous by our personal faith. The good news is that we were already born as perfectly righteous saints in the new covenant, almost 2000 years ago, thanks to the faith of Christ.

The Word of Faith says that God loves you

The word of faith teaching is based on attaining God's blessings in your life by positive belief, confession of scriptures and unwavering effort. After three years of intensively being immersed in this form of Christianity, it became a heavy burden. The "word of faith" became a "work of faith". It was all about confessing the right verses, rebuking the devil, commanding the blessings to manifest, etc. It became all about what I had to do, instead of just enjoying life and letting God take care of my problems and needs. Something is not right when faith becomes burdensome. That was when God started opening my eyes to His love that is far greater than my faith.

One of the important foundations of the word of faith is the Old Testament scripture where it says that **life and death are found in the tongue** (Proverbs 18:21). They emphasize that we must speak positively and claim the blessings. If we're sick, then we should confess that we are healed. If we're poor, then we should say we're rich. Now it is great to speak positively. But the word of faith teaching says that if we say anything negative then curses and death will manifest, but if we speak positively then good things will happen. It may have been true under the Old Covenant, but in the New Covenant, **Jesus tasted death to give us life by saying with His tongue, that IT IS DONE (Revelation 21:6).** If our blessings were based on what we speak, then it becomes our effort instead of Christ's finished work. The truth is that I have seen blessings manifest and prayers get answered, even if I complained and spoke negatively in unbelief. Our Father does not require His children to say the right thing or be perfect in faith. He loves us, no matter what we say or believe.

We are told to command the mountains to be cast into the sea and pray without doubting so that our problems will leave.

Mark 11:23-25 "Truly I tell you, if anyone says to this mountain, 'Go, throw yourself into the sea,' and does not doubt in their heart but believes that what they say will happen, it will be done for them. Therefore I tell you, whatever you ask for in prayer, believe that you have received it, and it will be yours. And when you stand praying, if you hold anything against anyone, forgive them, so that your Father in heaven may forgive you your sins"

Under the last generation of Jews, who were still under Law until 70AD, Jesus told them to have perfect faith. This was not just about praying without doubting, but it was also about forgiving others to be forgiven. They were not yet saved because the old covenant was still in effect. The Law was given on Mt. Sinai and this mountain was symbolically put on fire when Jerusalem was destroyed in 70AD. It was metaphorically cast into the sea, never to come back again. When Jerusalem was destroyed, the Old Covenant was destroyed, and salvation came.

Revelation 8:8 KJV "And the second angel sounded, and as it were a great mountain burning with fire was cast into the sea"

At that time, God made a new covenant where He does not remember sins anymore. Today we are not under the "word of faith" because it was required to escape the law. The faith and the law belonged to the old things in the old creation, and all of this passed away in 70AD. **Today we are in the New Covenant and New Creation, where it is not our faith or works, but it is all about God's love.**

We are told to rebuke the devil and keep fighting against him. Whenever we are in a traffic jam, fighting illness or facing opposition, then we are told that the enemy is doing it. I used to keep rebuking Satan for any problem I faced until I realized the truth that Satan was the Old Covenant system that was destroyed in 70AD. The finished work of Christ put me to rest that Satan does not exist anymore. God just takes care of things, even when problems come. **It's a big relief to be delivered from constantly rebuking Satan and confessing scriptures.**

During the yearly Thanksgiving holiday, Christians typically gather to thank God for the blessings in their life. In some cases I have seen that people are more open in non-religious settings, and they can be shy or afraid in more formal Christian meetings. But then, there are those who will use guilt to extract praise from believers. They say, *"Look at all the people who are dying and being persecuted. How can we not be thankful for our blessings? If we keep quiet, even the stones will shout praise to God"*. Now, I agree that we should be thankful, but we should not use guilt to motivate praise. God is not self-seeking, and He is not looking for the glory. He does not force anyone to give thanks because true thanksgiving comes from the heart. Sometimes people are struggling with problems, but they are told to offer a "sacrifice" of praise to God. Others are told to smile even if they are battling depression. I am sorry, but our Father is not a sadist and He does not expect us to be cheerful when we have problems. **He has no expectations on any of us because Jesus met all the expectations on our behalf.** Christ endured the cross with joy because He knew that it would save the world. When Jesus talked about the stones shouting praise in Luke 19:37-40, He was actually telling the Pharisees that they could not stop people from praising Him by their religious rules, because even the stones would praise God. It was not about forcing people to praise Him, but it was actually preventing legalistic people from putting restrictions on praise. Jesus blessed people even when He knew that they would not give thanks, but crucify Him.

Today, we can praise Him publicly or privately, without compulsion. It is OK if we don't feel like doing it, because He understands our problems. He is the most easy-going and calm person in the world. He puts no pressure on anyone, and we can be authentic and honest with Him, in all our struggles, because **He loves us the way we are and not the way we ought to be.** God does not look for our gratitude, but He is only interested in our well being, because He loves us unconditionally. It is said that the breakthrough in your life must be preceded by praise, or that you must worship God to see His glory in your life. All this was true in the old covenant. But in the new covenant, God has already blessed you with every spiritual blessing in Christ before we were born, even before the world was created (Ephesians 1:3-6). You don't have to praise Him to get blessings. Even if you curse Him, He will still bless you. Our complaining will not stop the Father's love, because He still provides for his children even if they are screaming and crying out loud. We don't praise Him for getting the blessing, because fathers love their sons and plan for their welfare even before they ask! If there is a breakthrough in our lives, then God has already ordained it before the world began, and it will come in due time.

Whether you praise God or complain, if you are confident or afraid, whether you believe or doubt, if you feel like it or not, whether you are good or bad, GOD ALWAYS LOVES YOU, no matter what you do. The Father's love for you can only stop if He stops living. Christ's love could not even be stopped by death. He lives forever and therefore loves you forever!

When problems happen in our lives, we hear that it could be due to many of these reasons. But I will show you that the Father's love is the answer to all these assumptions. We are told that God is testing our faith, but the truth is that Christ passed all the tests on our behalf through His faith; therefore we are not being tested anymore. We are told it's because of sin, but the truth is that Jesus took away sin and the Law almost 2000 years ago. We are told that God's ways are mysterious, but the true mystery is that He has made you righteous before you were even born. We hear that God wants our obedience but the truth is that Christ's obedience made us righteous. We are told to pray and fast more, but the truth is that Christ prayed and fasted, to endure the Cross and save us. We are warned to enter God's rest, or we may miss out, but the truth is that we are already in His rest, because He finished the work. We are burdened with more verses to confess, but the truth is that Jesus confessed three words

– *"It is finished"* (John 19:30).

We hear that God is breaking and molding us, but the truth is that Christ was broken on the cross for our restoration. We are told that we are in the wilderness, but the truth is that we are already in the promised land, because eternal life is not a final destination, but it is the knowledge that God loves us every day. We are told to praise and worship Him to get our deliverance, but the truth is that Christ delivered all of mankind from the Law in 70AD. We hear that the devil is attacking us, but the truth is that the devil was the system of the old covenant, that passed away in 70AD. We hear that our suffering is for God's glory, but the truth is that the Father never wants the glory at the expense of His sons. In fact, He gave up His glory to share it with us.

John 17:22 "The glory which you have given me, I have given to them; that they may be one, even as we are one"

We are told to pray more, but the truth is that Jesus prayed with sweat and blood to save us. We are told to pray in tongues to come to rest, but Jesus never prayed in tongues, and He has given us rest by saving us. We are told it's because we doubt His promises, but the good news is that even the "doubting Thomas" was chosen as an Apostle! We are told the problems are because of our lack of faith or works, but the Father whispers to us, "I love you, my beloved child".

God understands what it means to be human, because He lived as man. He does not even consider our fears, doubts or frustration but only loves us. God does not want to change you through your circumstances, but He wants us to know that His love is unchanging through all the situations of life. God does not take us out of the comfort zone, but He comforts us in every zone in life. He does not stretch our faith by sending problems to our lives, but He stretches His love for you from the east to the west, to put our hearts at rest. **When we cry, He cries with us. When we rejoice, He is dancing with us.** Whether you are a success or a failure in life, the Father is always well pleased in you through Christ.

Hebrews 8:9-10 NIV "It will not be like the covenant I made with their ancestors because they did not remain faithful to my covenant, and I turned away from them, declares the Lord. This is the covenant I will establish with the people of Israel …. I will be their God, and they will be my people."

In the Old Covenant, God turned away from the people of Israel because they were not faithful, and only a few entered the promised land. Therefore God made a New Covenant between Himself and the new man, Jesus Christ. In this new covenant, God is faithful to us, not based on our faith, but based on Christ's faith. Therefore our Father will always be our God, and we are always His children. **He is always faithful to us in the New Covenant.** When problems come in life, we don't need to struggle to hold on to His hand, because He holds us in His hands and will never let us go. We are held in both the Father and the Son's hand.

John 10:28-30 "I give eternal life to them. They will never perish, and no one will snatch them out of my hand. My Father, who has given them to me, is greater than all. No one is able to snatch them out of my Father's hand. I and the Father are one."

In fact we are engraved in their palms (Isaiah 49:16), and we can never be removed from His love.

2nd Corinthians 1:20 NIV "For no matter how many promises God has made, they are "Yes" in Christ. And so through him the "Amen" is spoken by us to the glory of God."

If God has made a specific promise to you, then He will keep it. The Father's promises are not based on our faith, but they are based on Christ's belief and faithfulness! When God made a new covenant to bless you, Jesus said "Amen" or "so be it". If He has ordained a particular blessing for your life then it will happen, whether you believe it or not. Sometimes we are told to strive in faith and come to rest, so that God's promises will come true. You are not called to strive in faith to enter God's rest because that verse in Hebrews 4:11, was written to the Jews telling them to overcome persecution in their faith, so that they could be saved from the wrath in 70AD. But God also told them, that even if they failed, His calling would not be revoked.

Romans 11:29 "For the gifts and the calling of God are irrevocable"

God's gifts, calling and promise on your life cannot be changed. Do you want proof? This chapter in Romans 11 talks about Israel, who rejected and crucified Christ. Even though they perished in the fire of 70AD, God restored their spirits and saved ALL Israel. He loves you whether you believe it or not. We don't have to stand in faith for Him, because it was Christ's faith that never wavered and attained the eternal life for us. **You are already at rest because you are seated with Christ in heavenly places.**

All those commandments to lay hold of God's promises, confessing the word of faith, entering His rest, not shrinking away, enduring in faith and not falling away, were specifically given to the people in the 1st Century who were transitioning between the Old and New Covenant. Today you are already perfect in the New Covenant because Jesus did everything.

The Word is Jesus, the Faith is Jesus, and Righteousness is Jesus.
The Grace is Jesus and the Love is Jesus.
We are simply the beneficiaries and the passengers.
He did everything and we did nothing. It is finished.
This is the new covenant. It is all about Jesus and not our faith.

<u>*We were saved by the perfect and unwavering faith of our Lord Jesus Christ.*</u>

Chapter 7

Universal salvation

We were flying back from India to California after spending Christmas with our parents. I was finding it hard to sleep during the 15-hour flight halfway across the world, but there was an unforgettable moment during this ordeal. I was watching an Indian movie, "PK". It was about this alien who came to explore the Earth but loses his GPS device that would have helped him return to his planet. He is desperately searching for it and ends up meeting several people from different faiths in India. All the people tell him to pray to God. So he ends up going to Temples, Mosques and Churches. But he gets kicked out of all them because of his hilarious but innocent questions that offend the religious people! There was this funny scene where the alien ends up in a Church, and he is shocked to hear that "God died on a cross". He panics and screams saying "When did God die? How am I going to get my GPS?" At that moment, the Christian Priest tells him to "repent, or he will go to hell". Unfortunately, this is the Christian Gospel that is preached all over the world – "Believe in Jesus or go to hell". In the movie, there is a scene where a Hindu farmer asks, "If God wanted me to be saved, then why wasn't I born as a Christian? Why will God send me to hell because I was born as a Hindu?"

Several questions began to arise in my mind over the next six months. If we treat people differently based on their religion, then isn't that called religious discrimination? And yet we preach about a loving God who sends Christians to heaven and everyone else to hell? If the Government of a civilized nation does not punish people just because they believe in a different religion, then how can our infinitely loving God do that to unbelievers? Would God send children to hell because they were Buddhists or atheists? Would He condemn the tribal man in Africa, who suffered all his life in poverty and sickness? How about those Arab children who died in the wars in the Middle East? How about the millions of Jews who were killed by Hitler? Would they end up in hell after their ordeal on earth? What about people who have never even heard the Gospel? Now, let's think of what we would do if we had the power to judge. Would I personally send my Hindu friends to hell for not believing in Jesus? What if my children became atheists one day? Would I send them to hell? No, of course not, how could I do such a barbaric act to the people I love!

The answer came to me – If I would not do it, then the God who is "love", will never do such a thing! God loves the world, not just Christians. He cannot be a God of love and a God of wrath at the same time. We say that Hitler was a mass-murderer, yet we justify that a loving God sends billions of people to burn forever in hell. Religion has messed up our minds! There are millions of people who never heard about Jesus. Billions of people have heard the corrupted Gospel about a Jesus who says "I love you, but I will send you to hell if you don't love me". Is that what unconditional love represents? Why would anyone want to believe such a Gospel?

Every religion on earth believes in this system of Law, where the righteous people are rewarded, and the wicked are punished, based on their unique definition of faith. Isn't traditional Christianity also similar to such an "Old Covenant" mentality, if we believe in this message of "Heaven or Hell"? Now we know that hell does not exist and that the "lake of fire" was the reference to the destruction of Jerusalem in 70AD, that ended the Law and the judgment of the world. Therefore, I believed that non-Christians would cease to exist after death. But as I searched the Scriptures asking God to show me the truth, I was amazed at what I found.

Adam blew it, but Christ restored it.

Christians believe that all people are sinners due to Adam, but that they are saved by faith in Christ. Today there are 2.3 billion Christians out of the total world population of 7 billion. So let's assume that all people were born as sinners in Adam, and if the world ended today, then Christ would have only saved 30% of Adam's race. This shows that Adam is greater than Christ because Adam was more successful in creating sinners than Christ could make them righteous. Therefore we are stating that Adam was universal in his sin, but that Christ was not universal in his salvation. But what does the Bible say? It shows that Christ was the greater Universalist than Adam!

Romans 5:15 "For if by the trespass of the one the many died, much more did the grace of God, and the gift by the grace of the one man, Jesus Christ, abound to the many"

It clearly says that "many" died due to Adam's one act of sin. But the gift of grace through Christ was given to the same "many". It does not say that only "some" received the grace of Christ.

Romans 5:18-19 "So then as through one trespass, ALL men were condemned; even so through one act of righteousness, ALL men were justified to life. For as through the one man's disobedience many were made sinners, even so through the obedience of the one, many will be made righteous"

Now this one is even more astounding. It says that "All" men were sinners because of Adam's disobedience. Therefore "All" men were made righteous because of Christ's obedience.

*1st Corinthians 15:22 "For as in Adam ALL die, so also in Christ **ALL** will be made alive."*

Just as all people were dead because of Adam, all of humanity was also made alive in Christ. When and how did this happen? It happened when Christ was raised from the dead.

*Ephesians 2:5 "God made us alive together **with** Christ (by grace you have been saved)"*

Jesus was born as the Last Adam and therefore he tasted spiritual death for all men. When Christ rose from the dead, all of humanity was raised with Him! Jesus gave eternal life to all of humanity.

*1st Corinthians 15:45 "The first man, Adam, became a living soul." **The last Adam** became a life-giving spirit."*

Adam's race ended with Christ. Nobody has been born in Adam since Christ finished the work on the Cross and removed the Law in 70AD. The entire human race is in Christ!

1st Corinthians 15:28 "that God may be ALL in ALL"

There are no more sinners. There is no more Adam or sin or Law. All of humanity is Jesus Christ Himself. God lives in every human being – in both believer and unbeliever.

The story of the Bible is simple:
One man (Adam) blew it. Another man (Jesus) restored it.

"God's will" or "Free will"

But then, we may ask this question. Did God save us without our free will? Let's find out here:

When Adam & Eve sinned, they never said sorry or asked for a savior. But God forcibly clothed the nakedness of Adam with the skin of an animal that was killed, which was a symbol of salvation through Christ's death. God told Eve that her descendant would come and crush the head of the serpent, and this happened in 70AD through Christ's 2nd coming. Neither Adam nor Eve asked for this to happen. God forced salvation onto the human race without their permission! Let's think of it. How many of us have accepted Adam as our physical ancestor? Nobody willingly accepted Adam as their "personal killer", because all men were forced into Adam by his disobedience, even if they have never heard of him or believed in him. In the same way, all of humanity was included in Christ and saved by His obedience, even if they did not believe in Him. We did not accept Christ as our Savior because He saved us almost 2000 years ago without asking us. He did it for us because He saw the need before Adam even sinned.

In Ephesians 1:3-5, Paul says that God predestined all people to be perfect in Christ as sons of God, before the foundation of the world.

Ephesians 1:9-10 "according to his good pleasure which he purposed in him to an administration of the fullness of the times, to sum up all things in Christ, the things in the heavens, and the things on the earth, in him"

God did this out of His good pleasure, to be fully accomplished on earth at a particular time when all creation would be one with Christ in spirit. In Luke 21:22, it says that this was fulfilled at the time of the destruction of Jerusalem and the Law that condemned all humanity. **That was the time when the will of God overcame the human will.** The will of God is Jesus Christ who removed the sin of Adam and the old covenant ministry of death, to make a new covenant that made all humanity perfect once and for all (Hebrews 10:9-10).

God blessed all families in every nation

God promised to bless all nations through Abraham's seed. In fact, God promised to bless every single family on earth through the descendant of Abraham.

Genesis 12:3 "All the families of the earth will be blessed through you."

The descendant of Abraham was the Lord Jesus Christ Himself (Galatians 3:16). It was through Christ that every family would be blessed. Christ took the curse of the Law, to bless all the people on earth. Through Christ, all of humanity has become the sons of God!

Galatians 3:26,29 "For you are ALL children of God, through faith in Christ Jesus ... If you are Christ's, then you are Abraham's offspring and heirs according to promise."

When Jesus died on the cross, He cried out to God asking why He had been forsaken. The truth is that the Father did not forsake His Son, but was with Him. God saved all families through the finished work of Christ.

Psalm 22:1,24,27 NASB "My God, my God, why have You forsaken me? ... For He has not despised nor abhorred the affliction of the afflicted; Nor has He hidden His face from him; But when he cried to Him for help, He heard ... And ALL the families of the nations will worship before You."

The Creator saved all creation – both believers and unbelievers

There is a question that is asked by some people who preach the Gospel: "Do you know if you will be in heaven if you die tonight?". We may quote Hebrews 9:27, saying that the judgment happens after death. But the truth is that this scripture was about Christ who took the judgment of the law upon Himself on the cross. When Jesus was buried for three days, He went down into the realm of the dead to preach the Gospel.

1st Peter 3:19 "in which he also went and preached to the spirits in prison"

In Ephesians 4:8, it shows that Christ ascended to heaven taking these spirits with him!

1st Timothy 4:10 "we have set our trust in the living God, who is the Savior of ALL men, especially of those who believe"

Jesus is the Savior of ALL people – both believers and unbelievers. Everyone will believe in Jesus either in this life or after death. There are two great examples of God saving people without faith. Thomas was a doubting unbeliever in the days after the cross, but he only believed when he saw the resurrected Christ with his own eyes.

Some ask the question whether "Hitler" is in heaven? The reason we ask this question is because we think we are more righteous than he was. If God saved people based on their works, then only Jesus Christ would be qualified. We don't focus on sins because Christ took away sin. We don't focus on works because Christ finished the work to save all of humanity. Religion loves to condemn both Hitler and the innocent Jews who were killed by him. But God is above religion. His thoughts are not man's thoughts, and His ways are higher than religion, as the heavens are above the earth. He sent His Word, Jesus Christ who accomplished the purpose of saving the world (Isaiah 55:8-11). If we want to know how much God loves the entire world, we can look at the example of Paul.

1ˢᵗ Timothy 1:15-16 "The saying is faithful and worthy of all acceptance, that Christ Jesus came into the world to save sinners; of whom I am chief. However, for this cause I obtained mercy, that in me first, Jesus Christ might display all his patience, for an example of those who were going to believe in him for eternal life"

Paul was an unbeliever in spite of hearing the Gospel and seeing the Apostles preaching all over Israel. In spite of seeing Christ and the Apostles, he persecuted them and killed Christians all over the Middle East, even as far as Damascus. He believed the Gospel only when he saw the glorified Christ on the road to Damascus. If God saved Paul in spite of his unbelief and sins, then He has surely saved all humanity! Every human being will believe in Christ one day, either in this life by faith, or after they die and believe by sight.

Colossians 1:15-20 NIV "The Son is the image of the invisible God, the firstborn over all creation. **For in him all things were created:** *things in heaven and on earth, visible and invisible, whether thrones or powers or rulers or authorities; all things have been created through him and for him. He is before all things, and in him all things hold together. And he is the head of the body, the church; he is the beginning and the firstborn from among the dead, so that in* **everything** *he might have the supremacy. For* **God was pleased** *to have all his fullness dwell in him, and* **through him to reconcile to himself all things**, *whether things on earth or things in heaven, by making peace through his blood, shed on the cross."*

Adam was a mere creation, and his one action plunged the human race into spiritual death. But the Creator (Christ) did a greater and powerful work! The Creator of all things has redeemed all of His creation. The Creator's work of salvation completely overturned the mistake of the creation. God the Father was pleased to make this happen. Jesus, who created all human beings, has saved every single one of them!

The Gospel of universal salvation

If all humans are saved, does that mean that all religions lead to God? No, the only way to God the Father is through His Son, Christ Jesus. But all men are already in Christ and are no longer in "sin" or "Adam" or "flesh" or "Law". So then, why should we bother preaching the Gospel? The truth is that salvation is not just about going to heaven. Many people of every religion (including Christians like myself) go through the struggles of this life not knowing that God loves them. They are not sure if they will go to heaven. They are under the burdens of religious expectation. Eternal life is about knowing the love of the Father and our Lord Jesus Christ right now, in this life. It is to live with peace, joy and freedom, knowing that God has already saved you. The Gospel is the proclamation that God loves you the way you are, and that Christ has taken away the sin of the world. The Gospel is not the threat of "believe in Jesus or go to hell".

The Gospel can be stated here:

"Even if you don't believe in God, He is your Father who believes in you. He loves you so much that He provides for all your needs because of Jesus."

"You don't need to attain salvation through good karma, good deeds or religious offerings. Jesus did all the work for you. God is your Father who lives in you. You have salvation now and not after a thousand rebirths. You don't even have to convert to Christianity, because Jesus saved you before you were born."

"You don't need to do good works or give up your life to go to heaven. Jesus is the Son of God who did all the work for you and He gave up His life to make you perfect and guarantee you the free entrance into heaven. God is your loving Father and not your judge."

"You don't have to go to Church, get baptized, do good works, endure in faith, confess & avoid sins, tithe, fast, or do anything to be saved or come closer to God. Jesus has done everything. Christ is in you. The Father is well pleased with you."

The Good News is that everyone will believe either in this life or after death, when they see Christ face to face and rejoice in His presence forever.

Even when we preach the Gospel, we don't need to do it out of fear by thinking that anyone's blood will be on our heads (Ezekiel 33:5, Acts 18:6). That was only applicable to the Jews who used such language to judge themselves by taking responsibility for Christ's death on the Cross (Matthew 27:25). Paul preached to the Jews in the Roman Empire, and when they rejected the Gospel, he said that their blood was not on his hands anymore, but on their heads. Such statements are not valid anymore because God has saved all people. We know that the Apostles were the eyewitnesses of Christ. They were sent all over the world, to preach to the Jews under the Old Covenant so that they could enter into the New Covenant. That ministry has ended in 70AD because salvation has come to mankind. But what about all the martyrs who gave up their lives for Jesus during the last 2000 years? I believe that they were never called to be apostles or martyrs in the first place. People in different religions have given up their lives for a cause that they believed was correct. We have also seen people give up their lives during military service in unnecessary wars. In the same way, there have been Christians who gave up their lives for the sake of the Gospel. Were their lives in vain? The answers are no. Even if they lost their lives on earth, God has given them eternal life in heaven, along with all of humanity. Heaven is not a place of regrets, but an experience of eternal celebration and happiness.

Now you may ask why this message of the 2nd coming of Christ and universal salvation has been hidden for so many years? I believe it is because God allows man the freedom to learn for himself. It was only after 1500 years when Martin Luther discovered that salvation was by grace and came out of the Catholic Church, so that he could bring forth the Protestant Reformation. As a result, most of the Church today believes that salvation is by grace and not by works. Therefore, will it be a big surprise that it has taken 2000 years for us to realize that Christ has already returned and lives in all humanity through His Spirit? If it will take 2000 years for us to realize that God has already saved all of humanity, then it's better late than never!

In Revelation 22:2, it says that Christ's presence brings healing to the nations. It happens when the world realizes that all people are equally loved as God's children, irrespective of religion, race, sexual orientation, economic status, capability or physical appearance. There will be no more religious strife, racism, or divisions. Then the world can focus on ending hunger, poverty, inequality, injustice and violence. Let this Gospel of God's universal love and grace, fill this world in Jesus' name.

Did God forgive all those who crucified Jesus?

Luke 23:34 "Jesus said, "Father, forgive them, for they don't know what they are doing."

The last prayer of Christ on the cross was to forgive the Jews who crucified Him. Now we know that Jesus and the Father are one. Therefore if God did not forgive all the Jews and if they perished spiritually in 70AD, then the Father and Son did not agree with each other. But the truth is that the Father and Son are of one heart – the heart of unconditional love! To understand this, let us see what happened when Christ prayed to raise Lazarus from the dead.

John 11:41-42 NIV "Jesus lifted up his eyes, and said, "Father, I thank you that you listened to me. I know that you ALWAYS listen to me"

Jesus said that the Father always listens to Him because the Father and Son always agree in doing good things. God the Father answered all of Christ's prayers, and especially His last prayer on earth! This means that God forgave them all!

In all the Gospels, we know that **Jesus came to seek and save those who were lost under the Law**. In the parable of the prodigal son, we know that the Father is loving and compassionate. He freely gave up his inheritance even before he died. When His son went away and wasted the money, the Father was still anxiously waiting for his return. The Father goes out of His way to celebrate when his son returns, without even asking him to confess his sins or taking account of the money. We know that this son represents the Jew who believed in Christ. But what happened to the elder son, who was a symbol of the unbelieving Jew who trusted in the Law? We see that the Father leaves the celebration and goes outside the home, to call his elder son. This is a clear sign that Jesus would do anything to save the unbelieving Jews. This is clear evidence that Jesus was successful in seeking and saving all those who were lost under the Law.

In the parable of the vineyard laborers (Matthew 20:1-16), Jesus gives the same reward to both the early laborers who worked very hard, and to the last-minute workers who barely did anything. This shows that all of the Jews were saved. He said that He would even leave ninety-nine righteous sheep and lovingly save the one lost sheep (Luke 15:4). Jesus was the also the one who found the lost coin because nothing can remain lost when Jesus is looking for it. If Jesus did not save the Pharisees, then He failed to do a good job. But praise God, that **Jesus was successful in saving the lost!**

He saved ALL Israel, including Judas, the Pharisees and the false Messiahs! But didn't Paul say that only the believing Jews (spiritual Jews) would get saved?

Romans 11:5,11-12,26 NIV "So too, at the PRESENT TIME there is a REMNANT chosen by grace ... Again I ask: Did they stumble so as to fall beyond recovery? Not *at all! Rather, because of their transgression, salvation has come to the Gentiles to make Israel envious. But if their transgression means riches for the world, and their loss means riches for the Gentiles, how much greater riches will their **FULL INCLUSION** bring! ... **ALL Israel will be saved**"*

When Paul wrote the letter to the Romans, in that time before 70AD, only a remnant of the Jews was chosen by grace through faith, and these Jews were known as the Spiritual Israel. The rest of the unbelieving Jews were not spiritual but in the flesh. But after the judgment and resurrection of 70AD, God had mercy even on those who were condemned to spiritual death! They were FULLY included in Christ, to fulfill the promise that "All Israel" would be saved.

The unbelieving Jews preferred to hold on to the Law, and therefore their bodies were handed over to Satan (ministers of Law), such that their flesh was destroyed in 70AD in Jerusalem, but their spirits were eventually saved (1st Corinthians 5:5). God had mercy on those who were spiritually dead and saved them because He is so good!

*Psalm 102:19-22 "The Lord looked down from his sanctuary on high, from heaven he viewed the earth, to hear the groans of the prisoners and **release those condemned to death**." So the name of the Lord will be declared in Zion and his praise in **Jerusalem** when the peoples and the kingdoms assemble to worship the Lord."*

In Ezekiel 37:1-14, it shows that God gave life to the dry bones of Israel who were dead. He poured out His Spirit to give them life!

*Acts 2:36 "Therefore let **ALL ISRAEL** be assured of this: God has made this Jesus, whom YOU CRUCIFIED, both Lord and Messiah."*

When Jesus died on the cross, we know that all of the disciples had forsaken Him, in spite of promising that they would follow Him. This included Peter who denied Him three times, and Judas who had betrayed Him. At that time, there was not a single Jew who believed in Christ! All of them fell away in unbelief. Therefore, "ALL Israel" included both the disciples and the Pharisees. In fact, when Christ died on the cross, the only one who believed in Him was the Roman soldier who declared that this was the Son of God (Mark 15:39). This was also a symbol of the salvation of ALL the Gentiles.

Acts 2:17 "I will pour out my Spirit on ALL flesh."

After the resurrection, on the Day of Pentecost, the Holy Spirit was given to the believing Jews and 3000 people were saved. But the rest of Israel was only saved in the 2nd coming of Christ in 70AD. In Zechariah 12:10-14, it says that the Spirit of grace was poured, in Jerusalem upon all the families and tribes of Israel in 70AD, when they mourned bitterly. At that time, they finally realized that this Jesus whom they had crucified, was their Lord and Savior. At that time, all the children of Israel finally came home to the love of the Father.

Romans 11:26-27 "ALL Israel will be SAVED. There will come out of Zion the Deliverer, and he will turn away ungodliness from Jacob. This is my covenant to them, when I will take away their sins."

At that time, Christ made a New Covenant with Israel, where He took away their sins. In Hebrews 8:10-12, the New Covenant declares that all of Israel would know God because their sins and lawless deeds would not be remembered anymore. This was clearly referring to the sins of "All" who crucified Christ. That was when He saved ALL Israel and ALL of humanity! What a loving Father we have! The law had bound ALL men as sinners, but He saved ALL men in Christ! Not one was left out.

*Romans 11:32,36 "For God has shut up ALL to disobedience, that **he might have mercy on ALL**. Oh the depth of the riches both of the wisdom and the knowledge of God! ... **For of him, and through him, and to him, are ALL things**. To him be the glory for ever! Amen."*

The Eternal Love of God

Psalm 30:5 "For his anger is but for moment. His favor is for a lifetime. Weeping may stay for the night, but joy comes in the morning."

The verse above has nothing to do with the new creation. During the judgment of 70AD, the spirits of unbelievers were separated away from the presence of God. The Jews had perished in the earthly city of the Old Jerusalem where the presence of God was no more. The presence of God was now in the spiritual city of New Jerusalem. But His wrath was brief, and it did not last forever, and great joy eventually came in the morning! At that time, the spirits of unbelievers were restored into His presence. Every knee bowed and every tongue confessed Jesus as Lord! (Isaiah 45:23) At that time, spiritual death was abolished for all peoples (Isaiah 25:7). The sorrow of separation from God ended, and there are no more tears of spiritual death (Revelation 21:3). God said He made ALL things New and not some things! All humanity has been saved, not one Jew or Gentile was left out.

*Isaiah 54:9-10 "**In overflowing wrath I hid my face from you for a moment; but with everlasting loving kindness I will have mercy on you**," says the LORD your Redeemer. "For this is like the waters of Noah to me; for as I have sworn that the waters of Noah will no more go over the earth, so **have I sworn that I will not be angry with you**, nor rebuke you. For the mountains may depart, and the hills be removed; but **my loving kindness will not depart from you**, and **my covenant of peace will not be removed**," says the LORD who has mercy on you."*

At that time, God made a promise to all humanity. His brief anger of judgment that came under the old covenant was now finally over. His mercy triumphed over judgment. He made a New Covenant of peace and everlasting love! **There is only one thing that is eternal about God. It was not His anger, but it is His love that endures forever!**

Understanding the Bible

If God has already saved the entire human race, then how do we understand the Bible? The Bible is very simply stated as follows:

Jesus Christ restored all that was lost by Adam.

The Bible starts with Adam and his sin, and it ends with Christ and His salvation. It begins with the Old Creation where all men were sinners, and it ends with the New Creation where all people are righteous. The Bible is about covenants. The Old Covenant made all men sinners, and the New Covenant of Christ made all men righteous. There is no more judgment or sin or religious rules, but people are discovering the freedom of the Father's love.

The Bible is a marvelous collection of 66 books that are inspired by God. If we interpret it correctly, then the result is peace, joy and love. But unfortunately, there are almost 40,000 denominations in Christianity because of the different ways in which we have interpreted the Bible. There are more than 3000 Bible translations, and there are a lot of subtle differences in verses, from their original Greek and Hebrew manuscripts. Why are there so many divisions in Christianity today? The answer will shock you. When Adam ate from the tree of knowledge of good and evil, he introduced religion to mankind. Religion is defined as a collection of beliefs on how to do good works and avoid evil, so that we can attain salvation. If we look at human history, religion has only caused divisions. All we have to do is look at the Crusades and the Middle East. Some denominations call their fellow Christians as heretics or false Christians because of differences in opinion on how they interpret the Bible. This is because we do not understand the context of the Bible. The truth is that the Bible was not even written to us. It was written by the Jews who were living under the Old Covenant. It was written to all the people under that Old Covenant, telling them about the salvation of Jesus Christ. It had clear instructions to them on what they had to do and therefore there was no confusion for them. They were called to forsake the Law and trust in Jesus because they were living in the final generation of the Old Covenant. Today, we live in the New Covenant where Christ has already saved all humanity. Therefore when we try to insert ourselves into the 1st Century Church and try to interpret the Bible according to our context, then we will have our own interpretations that result in divisions and heartache.

If we look at the Bible, it was fully written before the year 70AD. This was because all of prophecies of the Bible were fulfilled in the destruction of Jerusalem in 70AD by the Roman armies (Luke 21:20-22). Some people follow the red letters of Christ. Others follow every word of Paul, while there are some who swear by James and Peter. But the truth is that everything in the Bible has already happened. Today we cannot insert ourselves into the events before 70AD. God did not ask us to build the ark. He did not tell you to sacrifice Isaac. We were not called to leave Egypt, keep the Passover, cross the Red Sea and live by the Ten Commandments. He did not tell us to walk around Jericho seven times and shout to get into the promised land. He did not tell us to fast like Daniel or pray like Elijah. He did not tell us to cry like David asking for a clean heart. He did not tell us to sell all our possessions, carry the cross and leave Jerusalem. He did not tell us to do anything because Christ finished the work in 70AD. This is the reason why God has not added any more new books to the Bible. This is why the apostolic generation who witnessed Christ, ended in the 1st Century. If the Bible is about us, then God would have continued to add new books to the Bible and sent more Apostles for today. The proof that the Bible was not written to us is that the Bible has been completed and fulfilled in 70AD.

The Bible is about the journey of man from the Old Covenant to the New Covenant. Every book in the Bible was about events that were before the New Covenant was fully established in 70AD. Today we live outside the period of the Bible, in the time of the New Covenant. The Bible was about the coming kingdom of God, but today we live in the kingdom of God. The Bible was prophesying a new heaven and earth where there is no more Law or Temple or judgment. Today we live in that new heaven and earth where God dwells in us since 70AD. We are the New Creation that was fully revealed after Christ finished the work in 70AD.

We can receive tremendous encouragement and confirmation of God's love and grace in the Bible because it was not written to us to attain salvation, but it was written for us to know that Jesus has already saved all men. Therefore we can now stop arguing about all the Christian topics like: Law vs Grace, homosexuality & abortions, spiritual gifts, modes of baptism, tithing, losing salvation, Sunday vs Saturday Sabbaths, Israel vs Arabs, Catholic vs Protestant, Traditional vs Pentecostal, Spirit vs Flesh, Women preaching, Post-tribulation vs Pre-tribulation, Calvinism vs Arminianism, Full-Preterism vs Partial-Preterism and all other religious divisions. We can fight about the Bible for another 2000 years but the truth is that Jesus has finished the work and saved the world.

Acts 10:15 "What God has cleansed, you must not call unclean."

When Jesus destroyed the Old Covenant system in 70AD, He removed the separation of the Law between man and God. He also removed the division between "us" and "them". There is no more Jew, Gentile, Protestant, Catholic, Calvinist, Baptist, Pentecostal, Orthodox, Christian or Muslim. There is no more holy and unholy because all people are sanctified. Let no man call "unclean" what God has made "clean". There is only a new creation that is a new humanity. The truth of the Gospel is this: GOD is LOVE, and His LOVE does not keep a record of wrongs and does not exclude anyone. God has destroyed religion and its exclusivism in 70AD. He has included all of us in Christ!

John 5:39 "the very Scriptures that testify about me"

In my experiences of teaching the love of God, I have seen that some use the Bible to prove that God will judge the sinner and the unbeliever. They say that "God is love, but He is a judge". But we must remember one thing. The Jews were the masters of the scriptures, and they argued that the Bible demanded the stoning of the adulterer! They were correct according to the Law of Moses, but this rule is now obsolete because the Law has passed away and sin is not imputed any more. But Jesus told them something amazing: **The Bible is not about theology or rules or judgment**. But it is about JESUS–The name Jesus means "the LORD SAVES". The Love of Jesus said that the adulterer must be forgiven! This love demands that the He is faithful to the faithless! It guaranteed that all in Adam were made alive! The Bible is not meant for finding loopholes in God's love. It is not about finding out who is excluded by faith or sin. The love of God is greater than every disqualification in Scripture because it includes all people.

We may believe in the name of Jesus but don't believe in His nature. God is love, and He excludes nobody, but we have 40,000 denominations, and some of them hate each other. On the other hand, there are people outside Christianity who don't believe in the name of Jesus, but they believe in His nature. They believe in love, and they don't exclude people or call each other heretics or condemn people to a non-existent hell. It's funny and ironic, isn't it? The good news is that Jesus finished all religion and divisions. God has saved all people through Jesus. The Bible is not about KJV and Strong's Concordances, Greek and Hebrew understanding, but it's about the never-ending love and grace of Jesus Christ. In the end, the only thing that matters is this – God loves all people. We may not realize it now, but when we leave this earth, we will know that God is not about theology. **God is love, and love keeps no record of wrongs for anyone. The Bible is about JESUS. He is the lover of ALL people**. He is the Savior of the World. He has done it! All humanity has been made righteous in Christ. This is the Good News!

<u>Christ has saved every human being – past, present and future!</u>

Chapter 8

Free from religious rules

*H*ave you ever felt guilty for failing to pray, go to Church, read the Bible, or doing anything for God? Has your experience of Christianity been a never-ending list of things to do and not a place of rest and enjoyment? It's because of the obsolete religious rules that have come between you and the Father.

Christianity and the Old Covenant model

When we look at world religions, we see a common pattern. There is a holy place of worship where you go to meet God. This is the place where we conduct services to attain the forgiveness of sins. There is a priest or pastor who preaches from a religious book and mediates between you and God. This system of religion is administered by ministers who are supported by tithes or donations. This is the exact model of the Old Covenant that passed away in 70AD. Christianity can also be unknowingly based on the Old Covenant, and not on the New Covenant. Under the Old Covenant, the primary goal was to convict people that they were sinners, who were looking forward to a future Messiah. But we do the same thing in Christianity today, by telling people that they are sinners, instead of proclaiming the good news that Christ has already saved them and made them righteous. We need to remember that God never told Adam that he was naked but reminded him that he was made in God's image. The true gospel is to reveal that Christ lives in us.

Jesus came to put an end to religion by removing the need for a holy place of worship and mediators because He made us His Temple, where He dwells in each of us. Jesus did not come to establish a new form of the Old

Covenant system. Mixing both the old and new covenants can result in confusion, religious burdens and will eventually break down (Matthew 9:16-17). Through Christ's finished work, God has restored mankind to the place where Adam had fellowship with God, without the need for religion or sacrifices or temples. The New Covenant means there is no more need for religion. Today all human beings are Sons of God.

**The Church building is not God's house,
But we are His dwelling place.**

Does this mean that people should not meet to pray or worship God? No, we don't abandon it, because we are free to meet anywhere because God lives in human beings and not in man-made buildings. In the New Covenant, there is no more physical Temple (Revelation 21:22) because God is no longer restricted to a building with a priesthood. When Jesus was going to heaven, He told his disciples that He was preparing rooms for them in the Father's house. We may think that this is a big mansion in heaven, but look what Jesus tells them here.

*John 14:2-3,23 NLT "There is more than enough room in my Father's home. If this were not so, would I have told you that I am going to prepare a place for you? When everything is ready, I will come and get you, so that you will always be with me ... **My Father will love them, and we will <u>come</u> and make our home with each of them.**"*

The home that Christ was talking about was each and every human being. In the New Covenant, God's presence is not in a building on earth, or in a far away heaven, but He is one with us. He came down from heaven to make His home with each of us. God is Spirit, and therefore He lives in us, both in this life and after death. It's because we are one with Him in Spirit.

1st Corinthians 6:17 "But he who is joined to the Lord is one spirit"

So then, what was the Church? The word "Church" described the people who were called out of the Old Covenant to enter the New Covenant. The Jewish Apostles preached the Gospel, first within Israel, followed by Paul who went to the synagogues throughout the Roman Empire, preaching to the Jews and calling them out of the religious system of the old covenant. He went around telling them to stop trusting in the Law of Moses but to believe in Jesus, so that they could escape the wrath that was coming in 70AD, upon the system of the old covenant.

Hebrews 10:25 "not forsaking our own assembling together, as the custom of some is, but exhorting one another; and so much the more, as you see the Day approaching"

At that time, many Jews came out of the Old Covenant system but then stopped meeting their fellow believers, due to the intense persecution from the Pharisees. The verse above was written to them to continue meeting and encouraging one another in the faith till the 2nd coming of Christ in 70AD. Those who went back to the Law perished in the judgment of 70AD. Today there are many Christians who have stopped attending Church for various reasons. Some have grown tired of the traditional but powerless system of worship. Others have found Christianity too burdensome with all the religious rules. Some have tasted judgment and accusation when they failed in the eyes of the Church. Some have sown financial seeds, but have only seen the Church grow rich, without getting anything in return. But nobody can be accused of leaving because the Church was preaching about the love and grace of God. We cannot apply this verse against those who have stopped going to Church because it no longer applies to us. Today we live in the New Covenant where there is no longer a Church that must be called out of the Old Covenant system.

Hebrews 10:20 NIV "by a new and living way opened for us through the curtain, that is, his body"

Jesus made a new way when He died on the cross. At that time, the veil in the Temple was torn into two, indicating that God's presence was available to all men, apart from religious systems. And in 70AD, God destroyed the Temple in Jerusalem, thereby putting an end to all religious systems and making us part of His body. We are all the body of Christ because He lives in us.

We are free to go to Church if it blesses us, or not go there at all because God does not give us rules. There is no curse upon people if they stop attending Church. I personally believe that if people find religion too burdensome, then it's better to leave the Church and find a better alternative. The Church experience must encourage and strengthen us in knowing that God loves us and that Jesus has finished the work. The Church building is not the house of God, but a building where living temples like you and me can choose to meet one another. But this is not restricted to the Church building alone. You can be in God's presence with fellow believers or even with unbelievers at any place, day and time. This is because God is love, and whenever we experience love from our fellow human beings, we are experiencing the presence of God. I have seen atheists and non-Christians also display love and compassion, and this comes from God. He cannot be restricted to a building or defined only by emotional experiences like goosebumps, falling down, flowing tears, great sermons or religious rituals. He cannot be restricted to a certain group of people. This is because God lives in all human beings. Love makes the world go around because God is love, and He lives in every person, both Christians and non-Christians.

Sunday is not the Sabbath

For many Christians, the day of Sunday is a holy day, set apart for going to Church. Some believe that the Sabbath has been replaced by Sunday. But the truth is that we are not under the Law or Ten Commandments that were given to Israel. Paul clearly mentions in Colossians 2:16-17, that the Sabbath and holy days of the Law were shadows, but that the reality is found in Christ alone. The truth is that **Jesus Himself is the Sabbath**, in whom we have rest from all religious works.

Hebrews 4:9-11 "There remains therefore a Sabbath rest for the people of God. For he who has entered into his rest has himself also rested from his works, as God did from his. Let us therefore give diligence to enter into that rest"

When the writer of Hebrews, told the Jews to enter the Sabbath rest, he was not talking about keeping the Sabbath day, but to believe in Christ. The Jews were forsaking Christ and going back to the Law by trusting in the ritual of the Sabbath and the various other ceremonial laws. But Jesus is the Lord of the Sabbath. It's because the Sabbath is about resting from works. The Jews were told to stop trying to attain salvation by the works of the Law but instead rest in the finished work of Christ. If they did not enter His rest, then they would be judged in 70AD. Today we already dwell in God's rest, every single day. The Sabbath is not a day anymore, but it is Jesus Christ. We have found our resting place in Christ because He has already finished the work for us and saved the entire world. Therefore there is no more work for us to do to attain or maintain salvation. **We are at complete rest in Christ.** We don't need to keep any Sabbaths because the Law has passed away. Sunday has not replaced the Sabbath because God did not replace the Old Covenant with a new set of rules. He abolished all such laws in the New Covenant and gave us freedom. The Sabbath was only applicable to the old creation from the time of Adam till 70AD. We are in the New Creation where there is no holy day or Sabbath. We are free to go to Church or not go on Sundays. **The truth is that God has made us holy, and therefore every day of our life is holy.**

In Romans 14:5, Paul told the Jews that they were free to keep the Sabbath or treat every day the same. But they had to do it according to a firm conviction. It's because they would be judged if they had stumbled in unbelief (Romans 14:14). He told them that anything they did without faith was sin (Romans 14:23). The reason was that the Law had not yet passed away until 70AD. The Jews who were living in that time had to either keep the Law or trust in Christ entirely. There was no in-between. This does not apply to us today because there is no Law anymore. So there is nothing wrong with Christians who work on the weekends, skip Church, celebrate Halloween, practice yoga, eat pork, watch Harry Potter or celebrate other religious festivals. **We are free to do all things**. But if someone is weak in faith, it's better for his own peace of mind, to do things according to his own belief. But even if someone stumbles in unbelief, then there is no more sin or judgment, because it was Christ's faith that saved the world.

One of the things I also discovered, was how some people say that since we are in the New Covenant, then any special day like Christmas or Easter is not Biblical. The truth is that it does not matter whether those days are the accurate anniversaries of the event or just symbolic commemorations. The fact is that people just want to remember the wonderful events of Christ. We are free to celebrate Christmas or ignore it altogether. I personally feel it is such a wonderful time of the year when people of all religions in the world celebrate Christmas, even if they don't believe in Jesus. It is truly a miracle, and I believe that it is because God's love through Christ is hidden in their hearts. Some wonder why we decorate trees at Christmas? I believe it is a hidden reference to the tree of life. Christ died on the tree of the curse (cross), so that we were born in the tree of life having all those gifts, decorated in our lives.

Some people say that we need to keep "Christ" in Christmas and remove Santa Claus and all the gifts. Now even though I don't believe in Santa Claus, I can see that he is a symbol of our heavenly Father, who loves to give gifts. God gave Christ as the biggest gift to mankind. Thanks to Jesus, we can enjoy all these earthly gifts during Christmas and throughout the year. My kids love Christmas because they get so many gifts and this reminds them of our loving Father. The only difference between Him and Santa Claus is that God gives gifts only because we are His children, and not based on our behavior. I love Christmas because it's the time of holidays to be with family and friends, and give the gift of love to one another. That is the true essence of Christmas. It's not about religion, but the Father's gifts. During Christmas, we don't need to pray for Christ to be born in our hearts anymore. The truth is that Christ was born under the

Old Covenant so that we are born in the New Covenant. He was born in our hearts almost 2000 years ago.

Baptism

Should we get sprinkled or be fully immersed in the water? Do we receive the Holy Spirit after baptism or when we believe in Jesus? Should we baptize infants or wait till they believe the Gospel? Should we get baptized in Jesus' name or the name of the Father, Son and Holy Spirit? These are some of the disputes regarding water baptism. I have seen families divided and friendships ruined because of the disagreements caused by the different interpretations of getting wet in the name of Christianity.

Water baptism was originated from the old covenant. It always symbolized the washing away of sins and coming out of the old into the new. When the Israelites crossed the Red Sea by following Moses, that was their first baptism, and it was the foretaste of being baptized into Christ (1st Corinthians 10:1). It was how they escaped the slavery in Egypt, on their way to the promised land. When John the Baptist preached repentance to the Jews, he offered another baptism of water, to prepare them for Christ's coming. This was again a ceremonial washing away of sins because of the shallow and heartless way, in which they kept the Law (Luke 3:11-14). This was not the baptism that would save them because they were only saved through the baptism into Christ's death and resurrection.

1st Peter 3:22 NASB "baptism now saves you – not the removal of dirt from the flesh, but an appeal to God for a good conscience – through the resurrection of Jesus Christ,"

When Christ died on the cross and rose from the dead, the final baptism was commanded. They were dead under the Law, and they became alive by faith in Christ through the resurrection.

*Romans 6:4,6,23 "We were buried therefore with him through baptism to death, that just as Christ was raised from the dead through the glory of the Father, so we also might walk in newness of life... old man was crucified with him, that the body of sin might be done away with ... we **are not under law, but under grace**? ... For the wages of sin is death, but the free gift of God is eternal life in Christ Jesus our Lord."*

To be under the Law was to be in sin. To be under the Law was to receive the wages of sin. They received the wages by trying to attain salvation by working under the Law. But if they believed in Christ, they could receive the free gift of eternal life. Baptism was about being crucified with Christ and raised with Him. Being crucified with Christ was to die to the Law or stop trusting in the Law (Galatians 2:19-20). Baptism was for them to come out the righteousness of the works of the old covenant, into the righteousness of Christ by faith.

*Colossians 2:11-15 "in whom you were also circumcised with a circumcision not made with hands, in **the putting off of the body of the sins of the flesh, in the circumcision of Christ; having been buried with him in baptism, in which you were also raised with him** through faith in the working of God, who raised him from the dead. You were dead through your trespasses and the uncircumcision of your flesh. He made you alive together with him, having forgiven us all our trespasses, **wiping out the handwriting in ordinances** which was against us; and he has taken it out of the way, nailing it to the cross; having **stripped the principalities and the powers**, he made a show of them openly, triumphing over them in it."*

This is why Paul compared their baptism to circumcision. Under the Old Covenant, the Jews were physically circumcised, so that they were separated from the Gentile sinners. But at that time, the Law was coming to an end, and Paul said that the baptism in Jesus' name represented their true circumcision through the Holy Spirit. **This was how they were separated from the Law of Moses.** In some Churches, they tell the people to confess that they are forsaking Satan and accepting Christ during baptism. This was true for the Jews because Satan was a symbol of the Law that accused and condemned them. Therefore they were renouncing Satan by forsaking the Law to believe in the Grace of Christ. This was because Christ canceled the Law on the cross where the principalities and powers of the Pharisees were disarmed.

Baptism is mistakenly applied to repenting from sinful actions. This is why some people get baptized multiple times because they have multiple experiences of repentance. They get baptized trying to follow Jesus by repenting of some sins, only to repeat it again when they fail and repent. Now there is nothing wrong in getting baptized many times, but baptism was never about stopping sinful actions. It was given to the Jews to come out of the Law. Some people will say that if you were baptized as an infant, then you cannot be baptized again, saying that there is only one baptism in Ephesians 4:5. But the truth is that it was talking about there being only one type of baptism, in one Lord Jesus Christ and that too by one faith. This is because there were so many ceremonial washings and rituals under the Law that could never take away the sins of the Jews. But now in Christ, they were saved by faith in the final sacrifice of Christ that was represented by this baptism in Jesus' name. It was not talking about the number of baptisms in Christ, but the one type of baptism in Christ, as opposed to the multiple rituals of the Law.

Mark 16:15-16 "preach the Good News to the whole creation. He who believes and is baptized will be saved; but he who disbelieves will be condemned."

Jesus commanded the Jewish disciples to preach the Gospel to the Jews in the Roman world, telling them to baptize the believers. If they did not believe the Gospel, then they would be condemned. But those who believed would be saved. This salvation was from the wrath of the Law (Romans 4:15, Romans 5:9), which was coming soon upon the Jews in 70AD. It is fascinating that Jesus did not command Paul to baptize anyone (1st Corinthians 1:17) and Paul mentioned how this baptism divided the Church into factions. The reason Paul did not give much importance to baptism was because he was sent to the Gentiles, who were never under the Law and therefore did not have any previous ceremonial washings or circumcision. We know that Cornelius was baptized only after He received the Holy Spirit. Peter knew that the water baptism was meant only for the Jews, but when he saw Cornelius speaking in tongues, he said that even the Gentiles could be baptized. Therefore this **water baptism was purely symbolic for the Gentiles**.

Acts 2:36,38,40 "Let all the house of Israel therefore know certainly that God has made him both Lord and Christ, this Jesus whom you crucified ... Repent, and be baptized, every one of you, in the name of Jesus Christ for the forgiveness of sins, and you will receive the gift of the Holy Spirit ... Save yourselves from this crooked generation!"

But for the Jews, this water baptism offered them the forgiveness for their sin of crucifying Jesus Christ. They had crucified Him because they trusted in the Law of Moses. This baptism of repentance was for them to come out of the Law and believe in Christ. If they obeyed the commandment, then they would receive the Holy Spirit. They would receive salvation from the wrath that was coming in that specific generation in 70AD.

John the Baptist told Israel that Jesus would baptize them with the Holy Spirit and with fire (Matthew 3:11-12). The believing Jews were baptized with the Holy Spirit, with the evidence of speaking in tongues after they believed in Christ. But those unbelieving Jews were baptized by the fire of judgment in 70AD. Eventually, all Israel were saved – both believers and unbelievers–some through the Spirit and some by the refining fire of 70AD.

As you can see, this **water baptism has nothing to do with us. It was given to the Jews to come out of the Old Covenant into the New Covenant.** They had to believe in Christ through baptism and travel in the wilderness till 70AD. Today we are already born in the New Covenant. We were not born in sin or under the Law. But we were born righteous in Christ because of His finished work of the cross, resurrection and removal of the Law in 70AD. We don't need to get baptized with water when the living water is already within us. **All of humanity was already baptized with Christ** when we were all made alive with Him as He rose from the dead. He baptized us, and He did the work. Jesus has not commanded anyone to get baptized after 70AD because the Law has passed away. Today if someone says that we must get baptized because Jesus commanded it, then shouldn't we also sell our possessions and leave Jerusalem? You see how none of those were commanded to us. The new covenant has no commandments and therefore we have full freedom. You are free not to get baptized because Jesus already did it for you. You are also free to get baptized as a symbolic act in any manner – sprinkling or immersion, infant or adult, in Jesus' name or the Trinity's name, one time or a hundred times. God is already pleased with you, whether you get baptized or choose not to do so.

Confession of sins

When a person becomes a Christian, they are told that they are forgiven of past sins. But then they are commanded to confess and repent for any future sins. Salvation becomes a journey of uncertainty, instead of resting in the finished work of Christ. This is because of the lack of understanding of the covenants. The confession of sins was not commanded from the time of Adam till the Law of Moses. It was commanded for the first time, only to the Jews under the Law in Leviticus 5:5. This was because the Law made the Jews conscious of sins (Romans 3:20). The Law was given to them to make them realize that they were sinners because Israel was trusting in their own righteousness of works when they left Egypt. Sins were accounted for them as long as they were under the Law.

Galatians 3:24-25 NASB "the Law has become our tutor to lead us to Christ, so that we may be justified by faith. But now that faith has come, we are no longer under a tutor."

They were under the Law until Christ finished the work and brought salvation from the Law in 70AD. Once Christ completed the work, there was no more confession of sins because God does not remember sins in the New Covenant (Hebrews 10:17).

But didn't John tell the readers to confess their sins (1st John 1:9)? This is one of the most misunderstood passages in the Bible because we haven't understood the context. John was the Jewish apostle writing to the Jews spread throughout the Roman Empire. Among these Churches were false brethren who claimed to be without sin. John warned them about their false belief, because the Law clearly showed the Jews that they were sinners.

1st John 1:8 "If we say that we have no sin, we deceive ourselves"

These false brethren also denied that Christ came in the flesh. They said that Jesus was just another angel or spirit and not the Son of God. Such a teaching was called the "antichrist" because it went against the Gospel of Christ.

1st John 4:2-3 "Every spirit that acknowledges that Jesus Christ has come in the flesh is from God, but every spirit that does not acknowledge Jesus is not from God. This is the spirit of the antichrist, which you have heard is coming and even now is already in the world."

The Jewish Churches were filled with such false teachers who were the antichrists. They were living in the last generation of 70AD, in the last hour before the 2nd coming of Christ (1st John 2:18-23). Therefore John had to send this letter to the Jewish Church for two reasons: The first reason was to correct these false teachers who denied Christ. He tried to convince them that Jesus Christ did come in the flesh because John had seen Him, touched Him and heard His words of life.

1st John 1:1-2 "that which we have seen with our eyes, that which we saw, and our hands touched, concerning the Word of life ... that which we have seen and heard we declare to you, that you also may have fellowship with us."

He did this so that these false brethren would believe and have fellowship with the true believers. He told them that God would forgive them of all unrighteousness if they confessed that they were sinners and believed in Christ.

1st John 1:9 "If we confess our sins, he is faithful and righteous to forgive us the sins, and to cleanse us from all unrighteousness"

This forgiveness and cleansing was a one-time event and not something to be repeated all throughout the Christian life. We know that the Jews were forgiven of all sins, when they called upon the name of Jesus during baptism (Acts 22:16). At that time all their sins were removed. Therefore the commandment of confession was not to the believer. John addressed the false brethren in the 1st chapter of the epistle, and then he switches audience to the believers in the 2nd chapter.

1st John 2:12 *"I write to you, little children, because your sins are forgiven you for his name's sake."*

John tells the believers that their sins have been forgiven. It was a done deal. It happened in the past when they believed. They did not have to confess their sins anymore.

1st John 2:1-2 *"My little children, I write these things to you so that you may not sin. If anyone sins, we have a Counselor with the Father, Jesus Christ, the righteous. And he is the atoning sacrifice for our sins, and not for ours only, but also for the whole world."*

He told them instead, not to sin by going back to the Law. He told them that even if they committed any sins, then Jesus Christ was their counselor who made an atoning sacrifice for their sins and for the entire world. He told them that even if they sinned, they were still forgiven because Jesus Christ is righteous. There was not even a single Jewish believer who claimed to be without sin. How could it be possible for them to claim to be without sin and yet believe in Jesus who died for their sins? **Therefore the commandment to confess sins to God was not for the believer but only for the unbelieving Jew who denied Christ and claimed to be without sin.**

Confession has nothing to do with us today, and it was not even commanded to us, because we were not under the Law that accounted sins. We live in the New Covenant where there is no more sin. In the past, I used to feel at peace when I confessed my sins. This was because of my ignorance of the New Covenant. The guilt that I had was because my mind was trained by years of Bible knowledge, that told me to confess when I sinned. So I could receive peace only when I confessed my sins. My confessions and feelings did not make God forgive me. He already took away the world's sins 2000 years ago. God Himself does not even want to know our sins because He keeps no record of it. God is love and Love keeps no record of wrongs (1st Corinthians 13:5). He has made us perfect in Christ. He only keeps reminding us of the fact that we are sinless.

What about the Holy Spirit who supposedly convicts us of sins?

John 16:8-11 "When he has come, he will convict the world about sin, about righteousness, and about judgment; about sin, because they don't believe in me; about righteousness, because I am going to my Father, and you won't see me any more; about judgment, because the prince of this world has been judged."

The Holy Spirit came after Jesus ascended to heaven. When the Apostles preached the Gospel to the Jews in the Roman world, the Spirit had three convictions. The Spirit convicted the unbelieving Jews of "sin" and not "sins". It's because those unbelievers trusted in the Law that judged them as sinners. To be under the Law was to be under sin and it has nothing to do with us today. The Spirit convicted the believers of the free gift of righteousness, by reminding them not to return to the self-righteousness of Law, but to wait for the righteousness of God through faith, to be received in Christ's 2nd coming (Galatians 5:5, Hebrews 9:28).

The Holy Spirit only says one thing to you and me today under the New Covenant of Grace.

*Hebrews 10:15-17 "**The Holy Spirit also TESTIFIES to us…**"This is the **covenant** that I will make with them….I will remember their sins and their iniquities no more."*

If God TESTIFIED to us that He would never account sins, then He will never nag us or remind us of our failures. The word "covenant" means to make a promise or agreement. He will never find fault with us. Let's believe His word instead of reading the Bible out of context and applying verses that were written to the unbelievers under the Old Covenant. Today, in the new covenant, there is no confession for any human being because the Law and sin have passed away.

Repentance and Holiness

The word "repent" simply means to change one's mind. Under the old covenant, God told man to repent from sinning because the Law kept account of their sins. But when Jesus came, He preached repentance from trusting in the Law. The Jews became so self-righteous in their works of the Law that the Pharisees looked down upon the tax collectors, prostitutes and the lawless Gentiles. They were called to repent from their "holier than thou" attitude, and believe in the grace of God.

Romans 2:1-6,21,29 "For in that which you judge another, you condemn yourself. For you who judge practice the same things … do you despise the riches of his goodness, forbearance, and patience, not knowing that the goodness of God leads you to repentance? But according to your hardness and unrepentant heart you are treasuring up for yourself wrath in the day of wrath everyone according to their works ... You therefore who teach another, don't you teach yourself? You who preach that a man shouldn't steal, do you steal? ... For he is not a Jew who is one outwardly, neither is that circumcision which is outward in the flesh; but he is a Jew who is one inwardly, and circumcision is that of the heart, in the spirit not in the letter; whose praise is not from men, but from God."

Jesus had the harshest words for the self-righteous teachers of the Bible, but He also had great compassion toward the sinners. His call to repentance was for the Jews to stop trusting in the works of the Law and to humbly trust in what He had done on the cross. They were called to repent because the Day of the Lord's wrath was coming in 70AD, upon those who trusted in the Law of Moses. That day was the final hour of judgment.

Repentance today, is for us to know and believe that Jesus has already saved us. Religious teaching has corrupted our minds because it told us to become holy and righteous by our efforts. Repentance is simply the knowledge of the truth that Christ has already made us righteous before we were even born and He did this without our works or efforts. Repentance under the Old Covenant was to turn away from sinful actions because the Law imputed sins. Repentance under the New Covenant is to **turn away from self-righteousness** and the hypocrisy of judging others, because we are all righteous in Christ, irrespective of behavior. As you can see, such repentance is much harder for those who know the Bible and view themselves as more superior to the un-Churched or the unbeliever. I sincerely believe that we Christians act like the modern-day Pharisees if we think that we are better than the abortionists, gays, unbelievers and those whom we address as "lukewarm / backsliding / so-called Christians". This repentance will come when we realize that God has made everyone equally righteous as Christ Himself.

True holiness is not about being devoted to religious activities, quoting Bible verses, wearing the right clothes or avoiding jewelry and alcohol. **True holiness was the separation from the Law and its self-righteousness**. It was to be righteous by faith in Christ and not by trusting in the Law. The Pharisees knew the Bible, did all the religious works and yet were called the children of Satan. But Jesus said that the tax collectors and prostitutes became righteous by entering the kingdom. Today we are all holy and righteous in the new covenant because Jesus finished the work. You cannot become more holy than Jesus Himself. Those who say that you must be holy by trying to keep the Ten Commandments and the Sermon on the Mount are fooling themselves. If we really want to be holy by doing works, then we must follow Jesus all the way, by selling all our possessions and dying on the Cross, loving our enemies, without committing any sins in the process. **Attaining holiness by our efforts is impossible. Therefore we rest in the fact that Jesus has already made us holy**.

Some Christians say that the Law of Moses has passed away, but the moral law in the Ten Commandments still exists today. But the problem is that we cannot separate the Law into parts. Jesus said that not one bit of the Law would be removed until heaven and earth passed away, and all things were fulfilled. This happened in 70AD when Jesus removed the entire Law of Moses that included the Ten Commandments and the 600+ ceremonial laws. God does not want you to live by moral laws because the knowledge of good and evil killed Adam. God only wants us to live by the tree of life, which is Christ within us. He wants us to be led by freedom and not by ten rules written on a stone that brought guilt and condemnation (2nd Corinthians 3:7-9,16-18). Jesus has brought life and freedom by setting mankind free from rules and letting love lead us. Does a father need rules to be good to his children or doesn't he just love them naturally? No, he lives by love and not by rules. Only those under an old covenant mentality will think that they can do wrong things if there are no laws. It's because they need the law to reward them for good behavior and to punish them for evil deeds.

Religion needs laws and rules to keep people in check, but God has a better way called love, which is not commanded or threatened. The truth is that even unbelievers live godly lives without being guided by religious laws. It's because people are led by love and common sense. Love keeps no record of wrongs and does not force itself on others. Now if people ask if it is OK to do evil things because God has removed the Law, then it is a stupid question. We cannot sin against God or lose salvation, but we can hurt others by our actions. If we need religious laws to keep us from hurting each other, then we don't understand the love of God. When we know the love of God, then love becomes our nature. In some people, it takes longer, just like some trees take longer to bear fruit. In the New Covenant, it is God who writes his laws of love in our heart, and we just let Him do it in His time and purpose, instead of following forced rules.

The Lord's Supper

Like many Christians, I viewed the Lord's Supper more in fear than hope, because we were commanded to confess our sins before partaking in it. If we did not do so, then we feared judgment through sickness and death. But when I realized the truth about the Holy Communion, God gave me a lot of peace.

1st Corinthians 11:26 "For as often as you eat this bread and drink this cup, you proclaim the Lord's death until he comes."

When Jesus gave the Lord's Supper to the Jews on the Passover, He told them to do it in remembrance of Him. The Jews were familiar with the ritual of the Passover. Under the Law, the Jews were commanded to eat the Passover lamb to remember that God saved them from the death experienced by the Egyptians. It was also to remind them not to return to the slavery of Egypt. In the same way, the Lord's Supper was how the Jews remembered that Jesus was the true Lamb, who was slain to save them from the slavery of the Law. They took the Lord's Supper until His 2nd coming in 70AD. This was how they maintained their faith so that they did not perish under the Old Covenant in 70AD.

But there was a big problem because they were not taking the Lord's Supper in a worthy manner. It was not that they were unworthy but that they behaved like those who despised Christ. They were sharply divided and mistreated each other in drunkenness and selfishness while taking the Lord's Supper (1st Corinthians 11:17-22, 27-32). Therefore the angels disciplined them because they were behaving in a way worthy of being judged by the Law, instead of the grace of Christ. History was repeating itself. The Corinthians and the entire Jewish 1st Century Church were descendants of the Israelites, who followed Moses out of Egypt. Just like the Israelites spent 40 years in the wilderness before entering the promised land, the Church also spent 40 years from the cross till 70AD when the kingdom and the end of the age came. Therefore they were disciplined, just like the Jews in the wilderness (1st Corinthians 10:1-11). The Corinthian Church was a Jewish congregation that came out of a synagogue (Acts 18:8). They observed all the Jewish rituals like the Passover and the covering of women's heads (1st Corinthians 5:6-8, 1st Corinthians 11:10). Paul told them not to eat meat sacrificed to idols or commit sexual immorality because that was a sin according to the Law of Moses (1st Corinthians 10:8,13-14). Therefore they were still being judged according to the Law by the angels who punished every violation of the people (1st Corinthians 10:10, Galatians 3:19, Hebrews 2:2).

The Corinthians were disciplined if they broke the Law by despising one another. This is why Christ told the Jews to reconcile with their brothers before offering sacrifices (Matthew 5:23). If they broke the Law, then they fell sick and died early. James also told the Jews who fell ill, to confess their sins to one another and be reconciled (James 5:14-16), so that God would forgive and heal them. The 1st Century believers were being disciplined to avoid being finally condemned with the unbelieving Jews in 70AD. They took the Supper unworthily by worshipping idols, being divided and not believing in Christ. They were still under the Law where sin was being accounted, and they had not yet received the salvation until 70AD. This was because they were transitioning between the Old and New Covenants in the 40 years of wilderness between 30-70AD. **These warnings were not written to us because we already have salvation. We are not in the wilderness but we are living in the New Covenant where sin is no longer accounted.**

You see, the Jews were commanded to keep the Lord's Supper to proclaim Christ's death for the forgiveness of sins that they had committed under the Old Covenant (Hebrews 9:15). **The Jews took the Lord's Supper until He came and established the New Covenant in 70AD when He removed sins once and for all.** At that time, the Old Covenant and judgment passed away, and the Lord's Supper was fulfilled to bring the kingdom of God to the earth. The Lord's Supper is obsolete today, and it is not commanded to us because we were not born under the Old Covenant and therefore we have not committed sins. We were born in the New Covenant and therefore we have no sins. Where there is no Law, there is no sin. Christ has already come, and He lives in us. We have already received the full salvation before we were even born. When Jesus returned in 70AD, He made a New Covenant where He does not remember sins (Hebrews 10:17). **God does not discipline or condemn anyone today because He has saved all of humanity under the New Covenant.** He does not keep track of our behavior at all, and therefore you don't need to confess your faults anymore. Now, this good news causes us to live decently, loving others knowing that we are free of the judgment and wrath. Today, Jesus lives in you forever, and He is eating and drinking with us in every meal because the kingdom of God has come to the earth.

Luke 22:15 NASB "for I say to you, I shall never again eat it until it is fulfilled in the kingdom of God"

The Lord is not just with us when we eat or drink, because the kingdom of God is not about eating and drinking.

Romans 14:17 "God's Kingdom is not eating and drinking, but righteousness, peace, and joy in the Holy Spirit."

The kingdom of God is Christ within us. It is the knowledge that we are righteous because of His finished work. It is the joy of knowing that there is nothing for us to do and nothing for us to prove to God because He is our Father. It is the peace of knowing that we are loved unconditionally because He keeps no account of sin. Today we are feasting with the Lord in every day of our lives. We are feasting in the New Covenant (Isaiah 25:6-9) because the Old Covenant and spiritual death have passed away. Salvation has come to the entire world. The actual fulfillment of the Lord's Supper is that we can remember Jesus in every meal of life because He has made all things holy. It is not just the Lord's Supper, but every meal of our lives is a beautiful and holy fellowship with Him because we are one with Him in spirit. He made us holy therefore every meal is holy and a good gift from Him. When we eat food or enjoy life on any day, we can just say, "thank you Jesus" without any more fear.

Tithing

I heard a message a few years ago on TV, when the Pastor quoted the scripture below, telling people to send their tithes so that they could be blessed instead of facing curses and problems.

Malachi 3:8-12 NASB "Will a man rob God? Yet you are robbing Me! But you say, 'How have we robbed You?' In tithes and offerings. You are cursed with a curse, for you are robbing Me, the whole nation of you! Bring the whole tithe into the storehouse, so that there may be food in My house, and test Me now in this," says the LORD of hosts, "if I will not open for you the windows of heaven and pour out for you a blessing until it overflows. Then I will rebuke the devourer for you, so that it will not destroy the fruits of the ground; nor will your vine in the field cast its grapes," says the LORD of hosts. "All the nations will call you blessed, for you shall be a delightful land," says the LORD of hosts."

But was this commandment of tithing given to us at all? Under the Old Covenant, God had chosen one tribe of Israel to be a priestly tribe who ministered in the Temple. They could not do any other work. Therefore God commanded the rest of the eleven Jewish tribes to support them. The tithe was not 10% of their income but a tenth of their crops and farm produce. This tithe was then used to feed the priests and also the poor, widows and orphans. It was not meant for anything else. When the Jews tithed, then their own crops and farms would be blessed, but if they did not obey it, then their farms would be cursed. Now we know that this system of blessings and curses was only under the Law. In fact, if anyone did not keep the entire law then they would be cursed.

Galatians 3:10,13-14 "Cursed is everyone who doesn't continue in all things that are written in the book of the law, to do them ... Christ redeemed us from the curse of the law, having become a curse for us. For it is written, "Cursed is everyone who hangs on a tree," that the blessing of Abraham might come on the Gentiles through Christ Jesus"

We are not under the Law or the commandment of tithing. It is because Jesus Himself became the curse of the Law by dying on the cross so that the blessing of His obedience freely came to all men. Tithing does not bring blessings, and we are not cursed if we don't tithe. I have seen atheists and unbelievers blessed with tremendous wealth, in spite of not donating to any Churches. The sad thing is that some Christians who tithe their incomes also struggle with so many problems in life. This is because we are not under the system of tithing. God blesses people solely by grace and not based on how much we give to the Church. Jesus removed the Law in 70AD so that there is no more priesthood or Temple to support.

Today we live in the New Covenant where there is no distinction between the priests and people. All of us are equal because Christ lives in each of us with equal anointing. We don't need to pay tithes to pastors, but we can love each other and help one another, especially the needy. In the 1st Century Church, all the Jews left their jobs, sold their possessions and helped one another. They were specifically called to do this because Jerusalem and the Old Covenant system were going to be destroyed in 70AD. Therefore Paul collected food and money from the Churches all over the Roman Empire, to be given to the poor saints at Jerusalem who were suffering under great persecution and tribulations.

Romans 15:25-26 "But now, I say, I am going to Jerusalem, serving the saints. For it has been the good pleasure of Macedonia and Achaia to make a certain contribution for the poor among the saints who are at Jerusalem."

1st Corinthians 16:1-3 "Now concerning the collection for the saints, as I commanded the assemblies of Galatia, you do likewise. On the first day of the week, let each one of you save, as he may prosper, that no collections be made when I come. When I arrive, I will send whoever you approve with letters to carry your gracious gift to Jerusalem"

Paul never asked them to donate 10% of their income, but accepted cheerful donations of any amount that they felt like giving. There was a blessing in their giving because Jesus became poor on the cross to make them rich. There was no curse if they did not give.

2nd Corinthians 8:9 "For you know the grace of our Lord Jesus Christ, that, though he was rich, yet for your sakes he became poor, that you through his poverty might become rich"

2nd Corinthians 9:6 "He who sows bountifully will also reap bountifully. Let each man give according as he has determined in his heart; not grudgingly, or under compulsion; for God loves a cheerful giver."

Their giving was only to help the poor saints and not to support mega Churches. Today you don't have to sow a seed into any ministry to get blessed. It's because Christ Himself was the seed that was that sown on the cross to give us the harvest of eternal life and righteousness as a free gift. If He gave us eternal life freely, then He will also give us the specific earthly blessing that has been ordained for us, without sowing our seeds. If our salvation was a free gift, then every other blessing that we are destined to receive, must also be free and cannot be purchased.

John 12:23-24 NIV "Jesus replied, "The hour has come for the Son of Man to be glorified. Very truly I tell you, unless a kernel of wheat falls to the ground and dies, it remains only a single seed. But if it dies, it produces many seeds."

The tithe was also known as the first fruit of the crops that was given by the Jews in the Old Covenant.

2nd Chronicles 31:5 "As soon as the commandment came abroad, the children of Israel gave in abundance the first fruits of grain, new wine, and oil, and honey, and of all the increase of the field; and the tithe of all things brought they in abundantly"

Today, no one can accuse you of robbing God if you do not tithe. It is because the first fruit of Israel was the tithe. It was Jesus Christ Himself who was the first fruit! He was our tithe!

*1st Corinthians 15:21-22 "But now Christ has been raised from the dead. **He became the first fruits** of those who are asleep. For since death came by man, the resurrection of the dead also came by man. For as in Adam all die, so also in Christ **all will be made alive"***

Jesus became our tithe and first fruit. It's not your money or donations. He rose from the dead to make all of us alive. Tithing is not about giving money, but it is all about Jesus who did everything for you, so you don't have to tithe to anyone. If anyone is making money by using the threat of tithing, then they are robbing the children of God. Paul actually worked with his own hands to support himself and was not a full-time minister. He did not live based on the tithes and donations from anyone.

Now some will say that we must tithe to the Church because Jesus told the Jews to tithe. But if we want to obey everything that Jesus told the Jews, then we must also sell our possessions and die as martyrs. Jesus also told the Pharisees to pay their taxes to Caesar. For those who say that Abraham gave a tithe, we must realize that he did not give a tenth of his income, but he gave a tenth of the spoils of war after he defeated his enemies. He also did it out of free will, without any compulsion or commandment. If people are commanded to tithe because of Abraham, then please realize that he also left behind his home and gave up his only son as a sacrifice. We cannot pick and choose what we want to obey; when the truth is that none of it was even commanded to us.

We are not required to tithe anymore, but we are free to do whatever we feel is right. If you want to help the poor, you are free to do it on your own or through secular and Christian charity agencies without the burden of tithing. We are free to help Churches or ministries that are genuinely preaching the Good News and making a positive difference in the world. Even if some preachers are doing the work only as a career, God is gracious and helps them also to meet their needs. It is because those who preach the Gospel can work full-time and make a living through the same Gospel (1st Corinthians 9:14). There is total freedom in the new covenant from religious rules.

Prosperity and healing

The Law says that blessings come due to man's obedience and that curses come due to sins. The word of faith movement is also another form of the Law because it says that we are blessed if we believe perfectly and cursed if we don't. The word of faith movement says that all things are possible to those who believe and ask without doubting. To be honest, I have seen prayers answered, even when I wavered in unbelief. I have also struggled to see blessings come when I had great faith. The problem with the word of faith teaching is that it is completely based on human effort, and not the grace and love of God. Such perfect faith was only required in the old creation before 70AD. They had to believe in Jesus without wavering or going back to the Law. We cannot put the religious burdens of the law or faith on each other because both have passed away. Our blessings today have been preordained by God and given by His grace and not based on our faith.

Even though I believe that the events of the Bible have been completely fulfilled, I do still believe in healing and miracles. But I don't think it happens at the same frequency and intensity of the 1st Century Church. There are some of us who want to return to the days of "the Acts of the Apostles" so that we can experience all those great miracles. But the truth is that they were living in the great tribulation, where most Christians were killed for their faith throughout the world. That was the reason they witnessed such great power. Most of the Church today is living in peace and not under persecution. In 70AD, the judgment day was fulfilled, and the perfect love of God came and has already saved all of humanity.

Healing does sometimes happen by the grace of God, but not all the time. When it does not happen, people are blamed for their lack of faith. I have seen healing in my life when I did not have much belief, and at times it did not happen even when I prayed in great faith. I have seen faithful Christians, who confessed verses and commanded healing, only to die early deaths. I have seen Christians who stopped going to Church, and they live long healthy and wealthy lives. There are great ministers who can heal people but cannot overcome the common cold. I believe healing is the will of God, but we also do not live in a perfect world. If we could always attain healing by faith, then there would surely be some people who could have defeated death in the last 2000 years. But the truth is that both Christians and unbelievers have died in the last 2000 years. Healing and immortality are not guaranteed in this life. If it happens then we praise God. For those who died without healing, they are finally free of tears and pain forever, to be with the Lord. I personally believe that God also heals through the great advances given to medicine in the last 2000 years. Life expectancy has gone up tremendously, and infant mortality has reduced dramatically in the last 500 years. Doctors are finding solutions to all kinds of diseases with new breakthroughs. All this wisdom comes from God. I believe God heals through both medicine and miracles. It is because God is the Father of all human beings – not just Christians, but also every unbeliever and atheist. He wants to bless everyone equally.

I am not against prosperity because the Father always wants to prosper His children. Sometimes He blesses us directly, and at other times, He blesses the poor through their richer brethren. I don't have problems with prosperity preachers who say that God wants to bless us, because it is a positive message. It is definitely better than the cross-carrying, self-denying message of those who say that God wants you to suffer. I believe in prosperity and healing, but blessings do not come to us based on our great faith, tithing or good behavior. God's blessings are freely given in Christ and not based on our faith or actions. This is because I have seen Hindu Swamis, Atheists, Jewish businessmen and Christian preachers become wealthy.

*John 1:18 "No one has ever seen God, but the one and only Son, who is himself God and is in closest relationship with the Father, **has made him known.**"*

Eternal life is not a life without problems. It is to live every day, knowing that God loves us in the midst of this imperfect human existence. I have experienced suffering in my life when I was too legalistic and have come out of it realizing just how much God loves me. He did not send the suffering, but He always let me know just how much He loves me, in spite of the problems. We experience His love, both in good times and in bad times. When we experience this unconditional love, we will realize that we are not better than others. Many of our self-righteous ideas melt away after these problems when we realize that God loves us unconditionally and does not keep track of our failures. He does not say to us, "I told you so", but He tell us "I love you so". Some people suffer a lot more, but God gives them the strength to overcome it. For others who are weaker in heart, they receive a lot more prosperity, because God knows that they cannot handle the suffering. In the end, whether we suffer or prosper, it is only the love and grace of God that holds all things together. In the end, we will all be in heaven, where there are no more tears and death.

Jesus and not Job

When we go through suffering, we are not tested like Job. He thought that God gives and takes away blessings, but he was wrong. We know that there is no shadow of turning with God, who gives every good and perfect gift (James 1:17). Job also lamented that he did not have a mediator in heaven (Job 9:33), but for us, Christ has finished the work as our mediator. The truth is that God does not take away the blessings that He has freely given to us in Christ because His gifts cannot be revoked (Romans 11:29). Job offered the sacrifices for his own sons' sins, but he was confident about his own self-righteousness and even claimed that he did not sin (Job 35:1-2). The truth is that we already have Christ's righteousness and God is not tracking our behavior. The problems came to Job because he was under the Old Covenant, where he was under the curse of the Law. It was not God who cursed Job, but it was through Satan, also known as the Law. Job was finally restored because God found a payment for his sin, through the ransom of Jesus Christ's blood.

Job 33:24-26 "God is gracious to him, and says, 'Deliver him from going down to the pit, I have found a ransom.' His flesh shall be fresher than a child's. He returns to the days of his youth. He prays to God, and he is favorable to him, so that he sees his face with joy. He restores to man his righteousness"

Christ was the ransom for Job's sins. The Lord became his righteousness and Job was restored from the curse of the Law to the righteousness of Christ.

Job 42:10 NLT "the LORD restored his fortunes. In fact, the LORD gave him twice as much as before!"

We have this hope, that whatever has been lost in our lives, will be restored back to us by the Father because He loves us through the finished work of Jesus.

Holy Spirit

When it comes to the Holy Spirit, many believers think He is God's policeman who is keeping a watch on our behavior. But in Hebrews 10:17, the Holy Spirit reminds us that God does not account sin anymore. The Spirit always reminds us that we are God's beloved children (Romans 8:16). He always shows us that the Father has accepted us in Christ.

David cried out to God in Psalm 51:10-11, to create a clean heart in him and not take away the Spirit. That was only true under the old covenant, because they were not yet saved. The salvation of the Jews only came after Christ finished the work in 70AD. When the Jews received the Spirit on the day of Pentecost, it was a deposit of the full payment. They were sealed with the Spirit until the day of redemption (Ephesians 1:14, 4:30). That day of salvation was the resurrection in 70AD. Today we are not sealed with a deposit, but we already have the full inheritance as the Sons of God. We have perfect hearts and are united with Christ. We live in the new and everlasting covenant where God lives with us forever, and we are His Temple and body (Isaiah 59:21, Revelation 21:3, 21:22). His presence can never leave us because He has become one with us forever in the new covenant.

Ephesians 2:21-22 "in whom the whole building, fitted together, grows into a holy temple in the Lord; in whom you also are built together for a habitation of God in the Spirit."

Some people think that the spiritual gifts have ceased. But I do believe that the spiritual gifts like prophecy, tongues, miracles and healing do exist, but they are not as perfect or powerful as they were in the 1st Century Church. They still exist for us, so that we can bless one another. I have experienced healing at times and prayed in tongues. But it does not make me superior to anyone because we are all one in Christ and He is our greatest gift. I have also had people who prophesied events that came true later on, in my life. But there were times when the preacher was mistaken, based on their own personal interpretation. I can testify that if God has given us a prophecy or message, then it will surely happen. The promises of God are based on His faithfulness and not our belief or actions. Now, the manifestation of the Spirit is not just speaking in tongues. You have the Holy Spirit even if you don't speak in tongues, because even Christ did not speak in unknown languages. He only spoke the language of love and grace. John the Baptist was filled with the Spirit in his mother's womb, but he did not say a word in tongues. In fact, he was not even rich and did not heal anyone. He was in the desert, wearing rags and eating locusts and honey, eventually dying a brutal death. Not everyone has the gift of administration or organization. Not everyone knows the Bible and can give good words of wisdom. Not everyone can speak in tongues. Not everyone is merciful to the poor. Everyone is different with unique gifts from God. But whatever spiritual gifts we have, it is purely His grace and His working within us, and not for us to boast. We also know that the Spiritual gifts cannot be revoked because the gifts and calling of God cannot be taken back (Romans 11:29). If we give a birthday gift to a child, would we take it back if they misbehaved? If we as human beings don't take back our gifts, then God our Father, who is perfect in love and grace, will never do such a thing. He gives spiritual gifts because He loves us and not because of our merit.

Spiritual gifts are not just restricted to Christians. I have seen both believers and unbelievers speak divine words of prophecy and comfort, when I was going through problems in life. In the Old Testament, the Israelite man named Bezalel was filled with the Spirit and given the wisdom to build the Tabernacle of Israel. In the same way, God has given intelligence, wisdom and ability to people of all religions to make great advances in Science, Technology, Politics, Entertainment, Medicine and Sports. All these are gifts of God and the manifestation of His Spirit in all of humanity, because He lives in all people. We don't have to worry about the gifts and God's will in our lives, because He gives us both the desire and the power to fulfill it, by His love and grace (Philippians 2:13).

Fasting

Fasting is observed in several religions across the world and not just in Christianity. But when we read the Bible, the first instance of fasting was found in the Law of Moses. It was clearly an Old Testament practice that was done to repent from sins and plead with God to forgive them because the Law kept account of sins.

But what did Jesus say when He came to establish the New Covenant?

Matthew 9:11,14-17 "Why does your teacher eat with tax collectors and sinners? ... Then John's disciples came to him, saying, "Why do we and the Pharisees fast often, but your disciples don't fast?" Jesus said to them, "Can the friends of the bridegroom mourn, as long as the bridegroom is with them? But the days will come when the bridegroom will be taken away from them, and then they will fast. No one puts a piece of unshrunk cloth on an old garment; for the patch would tear away from the garment, and a worse hole is made. Neither do people put new wine into old wine skins, or else the skins would burst, and the wine be spilled, and the skins ruined. No, they put new wine into fresh wine skins, and both are preserved."

The Pharisees fasted a lot and separated themselves from sinners by keeping all the religious rituals in their Temple. But Jesus was different. He ate with sinners outside the Temple and went to the outcasts of Jewish society, like the tax collectors and prostitutes. He was always eating and celebrating with them. So the Pharisees questioned Him on why His disciples did not fast. Jesus said that the disciples did not need to fast when He was with them. It was a time of celebration due to the forgiveness of sins in the New Covenant. It was not the time of fasting and mourning over sins because the Old Covenant was coming to an end. **Jesus defined fasting as being under the Old Covenant while feasting was in the New Covenant**. Fasting while they were with Jesus was like mixing the Old and New Covenants. It was like believing in forgiveness and condemnation at the same time! The only time the believers fasted would be when Christ was away from them during their wilderness journey. But once He finally returned in 70AD to bring salvation, then there was no more fasting, but only feasting. That was when the Law was finally removed. We see that mentioned here:

Isaiah 25:6,8,9 NLT "In (New) Jerusalem, the Lord *of Heaven's Armies will spread a wonderful **feast** for **all** the people of the world. It will be a delicious banquet with clear, well-aged wine and choice meat.... He will swallow up death forever! The Sovereign* Lord *will wipe away all tears... Let us rejoice in the salvation he brings!"*

In 70AD, God revealed the New Jerusalem in the New Covenant. There was no more fasting, because the judgment was over and a new covenant was established, where all people were saved, and sin was accounted no more. It was party time! **Therefore, there is absolutely no need to fast from food. We can eat, drink and enjoy life, rejoicing in His salvation.** But before 70AD, Jesus told the Jews not to be consumed with eating and drinking like the unbelieving Jews who remained in Jerusalem. In 70AD, Jerusalem was destroyed like the earth was flooded during Noah's time (Matthew 24:38), but the believers fasted, prayed and watched for His 2nd coming. They were called to follow Jesus Christ by denying themselves, carrying the cross, fasting and praying in their wilderness journey. But the unbelieving Jews ate and drank, thinking that Jerusalem would remain forever. Paul told the Pharisees that their stomach was their god. It was because they trusted in the Law.

Philippians 3:1,18-20 NIV "Watch out for those dogs, those evildoers, those mutilators of the flesh ... For, as I have often told you before and now tell you again even with tears, many live as enemies of the cross of Christ. Their destiny is destruction, their god is their stomach, and their glory is in their shame. Their mind is set on earthly things. But our citizenship is in heaven. And we eagerly await a Savior from there"

Some preachers have used this verse to condemn Christians who eat, drink and enjoy life, warning them that the judgment is coming. But Paul was referring to the Pharisees who trusted in the circumcision or mutilation of the flesh, and persecuted the Church. These Pharisees were the enemies of the cross. Their minds were on the "earthly" covenant of the Law, the Temple and Jerusalem. But the Jewish believers were looking forward to Christ's 2nd coming in 70AD when He would reveal a heavenly Jerusalem, not based on the Law but based on grace. Today we can feast and enjoy food because God provides for our stomachs and there is no more judgment.

Today many believers practice the fast of Lent by trying to follow Christ's journey to the Cross. We try to imitate Christ who fasted for 40 days in the wilderness. We fast from meat and other delicacies, as a symbol of repentance and confession. But the truth was that Jesus actually fasted all food and water and did not trust in Satan who was a symbol of the Law. This is because He was overcoming the temptation of Adam who failed by eating from the tree of law. When Satan tempted Christ to turn the stones into bread, He said "No", so that the Father said "Yes" to us. The Father removed the stones of the Ten Commandments to give us the bread of Grace in Christ. He also gives us the daily bread and the needs of life. We are not called to copy Christ; otherwise, we would have to do everything exactly as Him, by never sinning, and dying on the cross as well. We should not dilute His words and try to follow Him when He never asked us to do so. His call for self-denial and carrying the cross was only for the Jews because they were under the Law. They had to overcome the Law just like He did. Carrying the cross was to stop trusting in the Old Covenant, and this has no relevance for us today. We are not under the Law, and we are already in Christ. We don't carry the cross because we are already seated in heavenly places with Christ (Ephesians 2:6) in His finished work. We are already complete in Christ, without the need for self-improvement (Colossians 2:6-9). **We should not mix the covenants by trying to fast, because fasting was only required under the old covenant. Today we do not need to fast, because Christ is with us and we are feasting daily in the wedding banquet** because we are one with Him in Spirit. He fasted for forty days without food and water, never sinned, carried the Cross and gave up everything, so that we do nothing but enjoy life and feast with Him every day. Fasting passed away with the old covenant, but there is feasting everyday in the New Covenant.

Luke 15:23 "Bring the fattened calf, kill it, and let us eat, and celebrate;"

When we read the parable of the prodigal son, we see that the Father provided a big feast for his son and did not tell him to fast. My children do not become closer to me or please me by fasting from their food, but in fact, we enjoy great fellowship when we eat together and enjoy life. If my children had to fast from food or the gifts of life, then I would be very sad! Your heavenly Father loves to enjoy life with you, in eating and drinking. Fasting was only for servants of the Law, but feasting is for sons under His love and grace.

Setting women free

Women are treated as second-class citizens in most religions. But this has also trickled into Christianity as well because of the lack of understanding of the transition of covenants in the Bible.

*1st Corinthians 11:5,9-10 "every woman praying or prophesying with her head unveiled dishonors her head ...... for man wasn't created for the woman, but woman for the man. For this cause the woman ought to have authority on her head, **because of the angels.**"*

*1st Corinthians 14:34 "let your wives keep silent in the assemblies, for it has not been permitted for them to speak; but let them be in subjection, **as the law also says**"*

Paul clearly distinguished between men and women and did not allow women to preach. He also told women to cover their heads. Was Paul a sexist or was it a cultural restriction? It was neither. He was just following the Old Covenant that was enforced by angels (Galatians 3:19), where angels punished every violation (Hebrews 2:2). The Jews were still transitioning between Old and New Covenants and angels ministered to them if they obeyed, but disciplined them if they disobeyed (Hebrews 1:14, Act 12:23). Paul preached the Law to the Jews but he did not enforce it to the Gentiles.

1st Corinthians 9:20-21 "To the Jews I became as a Jew, that I might gain Jews; to those who are under the law, as under the law, that I might gain those who are under the law; to those who are without law, as without law"

Therefore the commandment for women to cover their heads and to be silent in Churches was given only to the Jews because they were still under the Law. The Jews, who were living in the Roman Empire, needed to be reminded of the Law and not follow the Gentile customs. Otherwise, they would come under the judgment.

Acts 21:20-21 "how many thousands there are among the Jews of those who have believed, and they are all zealous for the law. They have been informed about you, that you teach all the Jews who are among the Gentiles to forsake Moses, telling them not to circumcise their children neither to walk after the customs."

When Peter told the women not to wear jewelry or braid their hair, it was a specific instruction given to the Jews who had already sold all their possessions. They were not given to the Gentile believers, because we know that Peter was the Apostle to the Jews (Galatians 2:9-10).

The good news is that the Law passed away in 70AD. Today we live in the New Covenant, where there is no Jew or Gentile, and there is no Law for us to keep. There is no male or female in Christ. No one is more superior, but we are all one in Christ. Women do not need to cover their heads or keep quiet because the Law has passed away. Men and women are equal. Both women and men are free to wear jewelry, tattoos and keep any kind of hairstyle. Women can preach in Churches and also pastor them. Today, we also see that some women are greater leaders than men. Some men can be mellow and feminine in nature, but some women can be masculine and aggressive. Some men and women have gay tendencies due to genetic reasons. These are not sins, because we are not under the Law that put women under men's authority. Today we live in the freedom and liberty of the New Covenant.

Prayer

Prayer is an important area of the Christian life and is something that I have spent a lot of time, experiencing and understanding.

The Lord's Prayer is very important to Christians because Jesus commanded the disciples to pray in that manner. But the more I tried to obey it, the more I felt burdened, especially with this part of the prayer: Jesus told the disciples that unless they forgave others, then God would not forgive them (Matthew 6:12). It was the most important part of the prayer and that is why Jesus repeated that specific commandment, immediately in the following verses (Matthew 6:14-15). It was an area I struggled with for a long time, until I understood that this prayer was not a New Covenant prayer. **It was the prayer of the Old Covenant.** I would like to show you that this prayer has been fulfilled in 70AD when the New Covenant was established.

1. *Matthew 6:9 "Our Father in heaven, may your name be kept holy. "*
   Our Father is no longer separated away from us in a holy place called heaven. Revelation 21:1-3 shows that heaven came down to earth and the Father is with us forever. In Hebrews 10:10, it says that Christ's sacrifice has made us holy. We are holy because the Father lives in us and with us.

2. *Matthew 6:10 "Let your Kingdom come. Let your will be done, as in heaven, so on earth."*
   We are not seeking the kingdom anymore because the kingdom came in 70AD. The kingdom of God is His presence with us, and it's the joy, peace and righteousness of the Spirit within us (Romans 14:17). The will of God was done in heaven when Jesus took away the sins before the foundation of the world. His will was finally done on earth in 70AD, because it removed the old covenant and established a new covenant (Hebrews 10:9-10) and made all of us perfect.

3. *Matthew 6:11 "Give us today our daily bread."*
   The Israelites were fed with the daily manna in the wilderness. In the same way, the Jews of the 1st century Church were in the wilderness for 40 years until 70AD. They had sold all their possessions and were fed by their brothers from the Churches in Corinth, Rome, Macedonia, etc. Today God has already given us His bread because Christ, the bread of life has given us eternal life forever.

4. *Matthew 6:12 "Forgive us our debts, as we also forgive our debtors."*
    The Jews were still under the Old Covenant and therefore were judged according to their works. The Law said that what they did would be done unto them (Matthew 7:1-2,12). If they did not forgive others, then they also would not be forgiven according to the Law. Jesus even told Peter that unless he forgave others, then God would not answer their prayers (Mark 11:25). He also told Peter to forgive his brother 490 times. The number 490 was very important to the Jews because it represented the end of the old covenant. It took 490 years from the time the Temple was built after the Exile, till Christ came and finished the work in 70AD. Jesus was telling Peter that their sins would only be forgiven in 70AD. When God made a New Covenant in 70AD, He declared that He would not remember sins and lawless deeds. God answers our prayers today irrespective of whether we forgive others or not. When we know how much God loves us, then we can forgive others freely without compulsion (Ephesians 4:32).

5. *Matthew 6:13 "Bring us not into temptation, but deliver us from the evil one. For yours is the Kingdom, the power, and the glory forever. Amen."*
    The Jewish Church was tempted for 40 years just like their forefathers in the wilderness. They were persecuted by the satanic ministers of the Law (Pharisees). In 70AD, the kingdom of God came in great power and glory to destroy Satan and the Law. Today we are not being tested, and we are not in the wilderness. We are in the promised land because Christ's faith has given us His glory and honor forever, by making us Sons of God.

Today we do not pray the Lord's Prayer anymore, but we pray in the name of Jesus. Now I used to think that we had to always say the name "Jesus", at the end of the prayer. That is not what Jesus meant. He did not give us a magic word at the end of the prayer that would unlock our blessings. **To pray in Jesus' name is to pray to the Father, as a son and not as a servant**. In the Old Covenant they were not the sons of God, but they were servants who had to pray according to their own merits of keeping the Law. But now in the New Covenant, Christ has made us Sons of God. Therefore we pray confidently knowing that our Father hears us because He loves us. It's about knowing that you are the Father's beloved son and not acting like a servant who thinks that the Master is judging him according to his works. God is not your boss, but He is your loving Dad.

When Paul told the people to pray without ceasing (1st Thessalonians 5:17), it was not because he wanted some people to become "prayer warriors". It was because they were living in the great tribulation just before the 2nd coming of Christ (1st Thessalonians 5:1-11, 23-25). He also told the Philippians not to worry about their futures during this great tribulation but to pray for everything because the Lord's coming was near (Philippians 4:4-6). This matches what Jesus told the Jews in Luke 18:1-8, that they should continuously keep praying because of the great persecution, so that Christ would come and bring salvation from the Law. **Today we are not called to pray continuously until God answers.** We are living in the New Covenant, where God has already finished the work. Whatever He has ordained in our lives, will come to pass. It's not based on our prayers or endurance. In fact, the power is not in the prayer, but it is the One who has answered all prayers according to His will. He is not moved by the length and strength of our prayers, but He is moved by His love for you.

Isaiah 65:24 "It will happen that, before they call, I will answer; and while they are yet speaking, I will hear."

God provides for us even before we pray, because we live in the new covenant. His blessings are not based on our prayers or faith, but based on His love, because a Father does not wait for the son to ask, but provides everything beforehand. He lives in us and knows everything we need. We can be at rest, knowing that He will always provide what we need, even if we don't pray or ask. I have seen God help me even when I did not pray or have faith. It's because He loves us and it's not about our faith. He knows the unspoken desires of our heart and answers them. Sometimes we think that God will only answer if we ask many people to pray together. The truth is that God is our Father who does not need anyone else to convince Him to bless you. He loves you as much as He loves Jesus and you are the apple of His eye. He will answer your prayer even if you have not asked anyone else to pray with you in agreement. The Father is in agreement with you, and that is all that matters. Demons do not hinder our prayers, as it happened in the case of Daniel or others in the Bible. It's because they were living under the Law when God was still far away from them. **Today we don't have to cast down hindrances, bind Satan or rebuke demons away from our prayers, because the Law (Satan) has passed away and there is no separation between God and us.** God lives in us and will bring to pass whatever is destined for our lives in due time.

If our prayers don't get answered, then some of us quote Paul by saying that His grace is sufficient for us (2nd Corinthians 12:1-10). That is because we have not understood the context. Paul was an Apostle who performed great miracles, but also suffered tremendously. Paul's thorn in the flesh was not a sickness or some accident. It was a messenger of Satan, who was a Jewish preacher of the Law. He persecuted Paul wherever he went, so that the Jews rejected the Gospel. But this is where God revealed His glory. For every Jew who rejected Paul, many Gentiles believed in His message. I have seen this in my life as well, where the persecution from legalists has resulted in the message spreading out further to those who need it. That is when God's grace is sufficient for us.

God is not stingy, and He does not find ways to say "No" to us. He does not demand us to change first before answering prayers. I have heard a saying that man proposes, but God disposes. That is so untrue of our heavenly Father. His plans are always for our good because He made us holy and blameless in Christ, before we were even born (Ephesians 1:3-4). If He gave us the greatest blessing before we even asked or believed, then why would He be stingy? The good news is that He is lavish in His love and grace. You don't have to close your eyes and bow your heads to pray to God. Prayer is just simply talking to your Father who lives in you. You can talk to with Him your eyes wide open or with your head held high. You don't need to take off your shoes, when you pray or go to Church, because that was only for Moses who was a sinner under the Law, standing on holy ground. He had to take off his shoes out of fear.

*Luke 15:22 "Bring out the **best** robe, and put it on him. Put a ring on his hand, and shoes on his feet"*

Today God is your Father who has put the shoes back on your feet and clothed you with the robe of His righteousness. He has crowned you with His loving kindness. You don't need to take off your shoes or wear a suit and tie when you talk to Him or go to Church. You can just be yourself because He loves you the way you are. God lives in you, and every place where you walk is the holy ground, with or without your shoes. You don't need to praise Him first, before He answers. He loves you, even if you don't believe in Him. Under the Old Covenant, God's presence inhabited the praise of the people, but now in the New Covenant, His presence is within you, whether you praise Him or not. You don't need to purchase His blessings because there is no cost. It is freely available without our tears, confessions, dedications and our promises. He listens to our selfish prayers as well, just like He answered Jabez in 1st Chronicles 4:10.

There are so many religious formulas and techniques that are given by preachers to help us unlock the blessings of God. They tell us to confess verses, shout Hallelujah, remind God of His promises and pray without doubting. We are told to confess our sins, pray with fasting, pray in tongues and pray for others first to receive the answer. We are commanded to worship God to see the deliverance, forgive others first, seek God and don't seek the blessing, don't ask anything but keep praising Him, thank Him first before asking, don't ask for wealth but ask for wisdom like Solomon. Don't you see a pattern in all of these things? It shows that God will answer, only if you do those certain actions. It is based on human effort and not God's love and grace. It makes your relationship with God like that between a manager and the employee. The truth is that God is your Father and you are His darling son. Does a Father need his son to jump through all these religious hoops? No, but the only time a child tries to trick his father into answering his request is when he is not sure of his father's love. Now I know that God still answers us in spite of all of our wrong beliefs, and that shows how cool and gracious He is. But **God does not look at our many words or techniques of prayer. His only motivation is His unconditional love for us**. In Ephesians 1:4-9, it says that it pleased Him to make us righteous in Christ, without anyone compelling Him to do so.

God loves all our prayer requests – big or small. He loves to hear from us. You can tell Him the most private, silly and embarrassing things. He's your Daddy, and He loves you. You don't need to keep asking, seeking and knocking the door from outside the house, till it breaks down. You are not the stranger knocking the door from outside, but you are the son living with the Father inside. Imagine if I told my kids that I would hide in my bedroom and only bless them if they came every Sunday outside my room, knocking the door, confessing all their sins, singing songs to me, and pleading to help them? Imagine if I threw them outside the home if they did not do all those things. What kind of father would I be? And yet this is the image of God that people have in their minds. Dearly beloved, our Father is far better than any human father. He takes care of our needs before we say or do anything, and we don't have to convince Him.

No more separation between spiritual & secular

Genesis 1:31 "God saw everything that he had made, and, behold, it was very good"

In the beginning, everything was good and holy in God's eyes. There was no sin in man because He was clothed with the gift of God's righteousness. But after Adam sinned, and especially under the Old Covenant, there was a separation between holy and unholy things. The Jews were holy, but the Gentiles were unholy. The Sabbath day was holy but the other days were normal. The Temple was holy compared to the land surrounding it because it was God's house. The Priests were holy compared to the other tribes. Certain foods were clean, but other foods were unclean. There was a clear difference between the spiritual and secular things. But now in the New Covenant, God has restored back all things to how it was before the sin of Adam. Christ came and saved all of humanity to reconcile and sanctify everything that was created (Colossians 1:16,20). The separation between the holy and unholy things under the Old Covenant has passed away. God made all things new in this New Covenant. In this New Covenant, all people, all places, all food, all days and all things are spiritual and holy because God dwells in everyone.

At one time I used to feel guilty about spending too much time enjoying the good things of life like sports or hobbies. It was all due to religious guilt based teachings that did not come from God, but from old covenant thinking. It was about the righteousness of "works" and "self-sacrifice" rather than just accepting that God has given us everything freely through Jesus Christ. The truth is that God never makes something good and then prevents us from enjoying it. God's hand has touched and blessed everything in life. All things are good gifts given by God for us to freely enjoy. This includes food & drink, being with family and friends, career, shopping, Church, vacation, hobbies, sports, that are all good gifts from God.

Going to Church is as spiritual as shopping because both are God's gifts to be enjoyed. Fellowship with God is not just during worship songs, but also when you listen to secular music, because God's talent is expressed through all types of music. We don't talk to God only during prayer, but also when we think about things in our everyday life. The presence of God is not just among believers but also unbelievers. It's because God's presence is not just about hearing a Sermon, praying together, crying, getting goosebumps and falling during worship. God is love, and His presence is experienced in all human beings who love you. I have known His love and friendship through unbelievers, believers, family, friends, coworkers and strangers. I have tasted His goodness on every day of the week and not just Sundays. God is not religious at all. He is cool, and He is looking at you with a loving smile. He is the most easygoing person you will ever know. He is the most accepting Father in the world. He made a New Covenant, where His presence is in every human being and every activity. Jesus put an end to religion by removing the Old Covenant. He made Himself part of everything and therefore all things are good.

Jesus has removed religious burdens to set you free

Chapter 9

God loves you

After hearing the Sermon on a Sunday in 2012, we were challenged to give up our "Isaac" and surrender something precious to God. I was already struggling with religion-induced depression during that time. The true image of the loving Father was distorted, and I viewed God as a taskmaster who wanted me to give up my career for Him. It was a far cry from the experience I had, when I grew up as the youngest child in my Dad's arms, who lavished me with such love and kindness. He never asked me to give up anything but was always the one who provided everything for me, at times even giving up his convenience. My earthly father was the foretaste of my heavenly Father's love. But unfortunately, religion portrays God as more of a judge and less of a loving Father. Now, thanks to the true Gospel of Jesus Christ, I know the loving heart of our Father.

God never wanted sacrifice. He simply loves you

The common knowledge in Christianity is that God gave the Law to the world as a moral compass. We are told that God consumed His anger and wrath on the cross because man failed to keep the Ten Commandments. It's almost as if Jesus died to appease God's anger and justice. But the truth is that God never required the Law or the sacrifices of the Law. It was never His will for man to be led by the Law, and to be under the judgment of the Law. The cross was not the wrath of God, but it was the LOVE of God. It says in John 3:16 that God SO loved the world that He gave up Christ for us.

The Law was man's idea of living by the judgment of good and evil. Adam started the ball rolling when he chose a system of justice instead of the unconditional love of God. Later on, Moses received the full written Law that required the sacrifice to clear the guilty conscience of man. **In Exodus 19:8, the Israelites asked for the Law because they wanted to live by it. But it was never God's idea! He only wanted to give His love and grace.**

Jeremiah 7:22 "For I didn't speak to your fathers, nor command them in the day that I brought them out of the land of Egypt, concerning burnt offerings or sacrifices"

When man worked under the Law, God gave them a sacrifice, not because He wanted it, but to satisfy their guilty consciences. Therefore Christ did not come to provide a sacrifice to satisfy God's justice or wrath. But He came to remove the guilty conscience by offering the final sacrifice of the Law to make all men perfect! He came to satisfy man's need for justice.

*Hebrews 10:1-2,8-10 "For the law...can never with same sacrifices year by year ... make perfect those who draw near. Or else wouldn't they have ceased ... because the worshipers...would have had no more **consciousness of sins**? ... Sacrifices and offerings and whole burnt offerings and **sacrifices for sin you didn't desire, neither had pleasure in them**" (those which are offered according to the law), then he has said, "**Behold, I have come to do your will.**" He takes away the first, that he may establish the second, **by which will we have been sanctified through the offering of the body of Jesus Christ once for all.**"*

The will of God, was not for man to keep rules and laws, but it was to remove the Law and make humanity perfect because of His great love! But some will quote Isaiah 53:10 and say that it pleased God to see Christ die on the cross. But, our Father is not like that at all. Is there any father who likes to see his son dying so brutally? The Father was pleased, not because it supposedly satisfied His wrath, but because it was His love that was displayed on the Cross!

Ephesians 5:2 "Christ also loved you, and gave himself up for us, an offering and a sacrifice to God for a sweet-smelling fragrance"

The death of Christ was not about Jesus pacifying an angry God. But it was Jesus doing what He saw the Father doing Himself. It was the greatest display of LOVE!

John 5:19 "the Son can do nothing of himself, but what he sees the Father doing. For whatever things he does, these the Son also does likewise."

When Jesus washed the feet of the disciples with a humble heart, it was because that is what the Father does. When Jesus forgave those who crucified Him, it was the expression of the Father's loving heart. When Jesus went out of His way to heal the sick and forgive people, it was the Father doing it through the Son.

2nd Corinthians 5:14,19 "The LOVE of Christ … God was IN Christ reconciling the world to himself, not reckoning to them their trespasses"

When Jesus loved us by dying on the cross, it was because that is what the Father was doing in Christ and through Him. The Father and Son are of one heart. The Father is Love! The Son is Love! The Spirit is Love! When Jesus died on the cross, the Father was IN the Son, on the cross, displaying His great LOVE that took away the sins of the world. It was not a display of God's justice, but His great love.

God is love, without ifs and buts

We hear that God is love but that He also has wrath and judgment. We are told that God is love, but that He is just and must punish the wicked. But how can we say that love keeps no record of wrongs, and yet still declare that He will judge people today? We have created a bipolar God according to our ideas. The reason we see judgment and wrath in the Bible is because man had put himself in the system of the knowledge of good and evil. Adam chose this system of law, where man would be judged by his performance. Therefore God had no choice but to honor the free will of man. This is why we see the destruction of Sodom, Noah's flood and all the judgments on Israel throughout the Bible. The Law judged the old creation because it accounted sin and rewarded good works.

But as we know, that God never desired the law or its sacrifices. This clearly shows that He never wanted to bring judgment. The Bible says that God is love (1st John 4:8), and we know that love does not take revenge on others or treat others according to what they deserve. God has always been love, and He has never been wrathful or judgmental. As long as the world was under the Law, God had to honor the Law. But once Christ came and took away the Law, He revealed the true face of God – the loving Father who has always loved His sons. That is why God said that the old order has passed away and that He was making all things new (Revelation 21:3-4). The new covenant of His love and grace has always been His true image, where He does not account sins. The new covenant has always been God's plan because it is called the everlasting covenant. His love has been eternal, even though it has seemed new to man. This was because we have always related to God based on our flawed thinking of the law. **God is not "Law"** but God is **"Love"**. There are no "ifs and buts" with God's love. His love endures forever because He was never about wrath, but always about love.

God's will and surrender

So much of Christian teaching tells us to offer up our sacrifices to God, just like how Abraham offered Isaac. It tells us to give up our desires, plans, careers and hobbies to please God. But God does not want any such sacrifice. He only wants us to know that He sacrificed Himself because He loves us. When Abraham sacrificed his only son Isaac, it was a foretaste of the only Son of God, Jesus who died on the cross because of His great love for us. The Father has never demanded anything from us. Any such demand is from religion that caters to man's self-righteousness and not the free gift of God's righteousness.

The famous passage in Romans 12:1-2 apparently tells people to please God by offering living sacrifices, not conforming to the world. Christians are told to surrender their time, money and resources to please God. But let us ask ourselves this question – does a father demand such things from his children? I don't know any good father who does this. But instead, he always fulfills the desires of his children! If God did not ask us for any sacrifice, then what was the meaning of this passage? We will find that Paul was writing to Jews in Rome, who were coming out of the Old Covenant. He wrote eleven chapters to them, explaining how righteousness was not obtained by the sacrifices of the Law, but by the faith of Christ's finished work. The "world" was referring to the Old Covenant system that they were not supposed to conform to anymore. He explains this in the letter to the Galatians, telling them not to go back to the worldly principles of the Law.

*Galatians 4:3,5,9-10 "So we also, when we were children, were held in bondage under the **elemental principles of the world** ... that He might redeem those who were **under the law** ... But now that you have come to know God or rather to be known by God, **why do you turn back again to the weak and miserable elemental principles**, to which you desire to be in bondage all over again? You observe days, months, seasons and years."*

He told all the Churches, to have faith in Christ and not return to the old covenant so that they could escape the wrath that was coming in 70AD. So in view of God's great mercy, he pleaded with them, to stop trusting in the dead sacrifice of the Law, but to trust in the living sacrifice of Christ, who lives forever! **Today your Father is not asking you to offer any sacrifice or escape the world, because Christ the living sacrifice, is already living**

in you. He is telling us today to stop offering our self-righteous works of surrender and sacrifice, and know the truth that we are already righteous because of Christ's sacrifice. We have already escaped the world of the Old Covenant system because it came to an end in 70AD. You don't need to do anything, because He has already done everything, and has freely given you life to enjoy in the new covenant world.

For many Christians, finding the will of God can be nerve-wracking, because we are afraid of what we need to do to please Him. I spent a lot of time trying to surrender my career for God, which led me into depression because I failed in my efforts. I thought that I could never please God by faith and was going to lose my salvation. But the truth is that God does not put any religious burden on us. He is not a harsh taskmaster, but your loving Father who delights in you. So what is God's will for your life? In Hebrews 10:8-10, it shows us that the will of God was to remove the old covenant and all its demands so that He made a new covenant where Jesus did everything for us and made us perfect forever. Under the old covenant, man said this to God, *"I will do everything you say"*. But man could not do it, and he was unfaithful. Therefore God sent Christ to do everything for us and take away this old covenant system. In the new covenant, we can say this *"Father; thank you that Jesus has done everything. Your will is that I naturally follow the desire and passion of my heart. You are happy when I am happy."*

The will of God was not about our faith, sacrifices, surrender or works. The will of God was that He Himself came as a man and displayed perfect faith and works to take away the Old Covenant of rules and regulations. **God's will was to establish the New Covenant so that we have been made perfect, once and for all. The will of God is that you do nothing because He has done everything.** The will of God is that you know this truth about His unconditional love. The will of God is that He took away all sin, laws and the judgment. There is no more sin and no more expectation on you. He is completely pleased in you because of what Jesus has done.

When Jesus was going to the cross, He told the Father "not my will, but yours be done". Jesus gave up His desires and His will, so that we may enjoy the Father's love and the abundant life. We are not called to follow Jesus to the cross by giving up our desires because He surrendered His life for you. He sacrificed Himself under the Law so that He fulfills the desires of our heart, by Grace.

Philippians 2:13 NLT "For God is working in you, giving you the desire and the power to do what pleases him."

When God gives you the desire, He also gives the power to do it, and you are always pleasing to Him, because He gave us those desires and the works, before the world began (Ephesians 2:10).

God is not asking you to sacrifice your weekend by going to Church. He is not asking you to spend one hour of prayer. He is not asking you to give up a meal by fasting. He is not asking you to surrender your life for the Gospel. He is not asking you to give a tithe. Jesus has done everything for us already. If you are doing things out of compulsion, fear, obligation, guilt or pressure, then you can be sure that it's not the will of God. But if you are doing anything from your heart, because you love to do so, without compulsion, fear or pride, then you know that it is God who is doing it within you.

*Isaiah 55:9-12 NASB "For as the heavens are higher than the earth, So are My ways higher than your ways And My thoughts than your thoughts. "For as the rain and the snow come down from heaven, And do not return there without watering the earth And making it bear and sprout, And furnishing seed to the sower and bread to the eater; So will My word be which goes forth from My mouth; It will not return to Me empty, Without accomplishing what I desire, And without succeeding in the matter for which I sent it. "**For you will go out with joy And be led forth with peace;**"*

God's thoughts are much higher than man's thoughts. We may think that we are pleasing God, by asking Him to tell us what to do. But that is a form of old covenant thinking, where we need rules to follow. This is the mind of the flesh, where there is no peace but a sense of compulsion with either pride or guilt (Romans 8:6). This is performance-driven Christianity; that is a form of servanthood and slavery. This originates from the minds of men, where we can never please God because we will always fall short of the demands created in our mind. But the new covenant life of freedom and son-ship is about doing what God has placed in your heart. It is the mind of the Spirit, where we know that we are beloved sons of God, who are already pleasing to Him. You don't have to apply Jeremiah 17:9 to yourself. That verse told the Jews that they had desperately wicked and deceitful hearts under the old covenant. Today you already have a new heart that is pure under the new covenant (Ezekiel 36:26, Acts 15:9). **The Father says that He has already sent the Word to the earth to accomplish His purpose.** The Word was Jesus Himself, who came to the earth and finished the work in 70AD, having saved all of humanity. **The will of God in your life is Jesus Christ who did everything for you.** He made us righteous without any of our efforts to surrender or sacrifice our lives. The knowledge of this truth will give us peace and joy to enjoy our lives and follow our hearts. Truly His thoughts are unimaginably good, resulting in love, grace and peace in our hearts.

The Kingdom is within you

We have heard that God will take care of our needs only if we first seek God's kingdom and give importance to Christian activities. That's like a father telling his children that he will provide food for them, only if they give top priority to his business or career. I know that does not sound right. So then, what did Jesus mean by seeking the kingdom?

*Luke 12:31-40 "But **seek God's Kingdom**, and all these things will be added to you. Don't be afraid, little flock, for it is your Father's good pleasure to give you the Kingdom. **Sell that which you have**, and give gifts to the needy. Make for yourselves purses which don't grow old, a treasure in the heavens that doesn't fail, where no thief approaches, neither moth destroys. For where your treasure is, there will your heart be also. "Let your waist be dressed and your lamps burning. **Be like men watching for their lord**, when he returns from the marriage feast; that, when he comes and knocks, they may immediately open to him. Blessed are those servants, whom the lord will find watching when he comes. Most certainly I tell you, that he will dress himself, and make them recline, and will come and serve them. They will be blessed if he comes in the second or third watch, and finds them so. But know this, that if the master of the house had known in what hour **the thief was coming**, he would have watched, and not allowed his house to be broken into. Therefore **be ready also**, for the Son of Man is coming in an hour that you don't expect him."*

Jesus told the Jews to sell all their possessions and give to the poor because the kingdom of God was coming. He told them to forsake the Old Covenant kingdom of Israel and be ready for the New Covenant kingdom of the Spirit. They were called to leave behind their jobs and their homes in Israel so that they could enter the kingdom. This was because Israel was going to be destroyed in 70AD when Christ returned in His 2nd coming. He told them to sell everything and not to trust in the perishing riches of Israel because His coming would be like a thief who destroyed those riches in 70AD. They obeyed and received the inheritance of eternal life in the kingdom.

Colossians 1:13-14 "who delivered us out of the power of darkness, and translated us into the Kingdom of the Son of his love; in whom we have our redemption, the forgiveness of our sins"

The Old Covenant was the power of darkness. This was why Christ told them to follow the light of His grace and come out of the darkness of the Law (John 12:46). The believers were transferred into the Kingdom of God by the finished work of Christ when He forgave their sins and all of humanity. The kingdom of God was not found in the religion of the Jews and the laws that demanded the righteousness of works. But the kingdom of God is the knowledge that He has made us righteous in Christ, apart from any works. Today, we are already born in the new covenant kingdom of God, because the Law does not exist anymore, thanks to Jesus Christ.

*Luke 17:20-21 "Being asked by the Pharisees when God's Kingdom would come, he answered them, "God's Kingdom doesn't come with observation; neither will they say, 'Look, here!' or, 'Look, there!' for behold, **God's Kingdom is within you.**"*

The kingdom of God is not a place in outer space. In 70AD, the kingdom of God came to this earth when the Spirit of God was poured out on all humanity. Today Jesus is with us, and He lives in us. It is righteousness, joy and peace in the Holy Spirit who dwells in you (Romans 14:17). You already have the kingdom, and you don't have to give up anything to attain it. The king lives in you, and He has made you His kingdom. The kingdom is not a place, but it is a person – Jesus Christ who lives in you. You don't have to become righteous by your personal faith or works because Jesus Himself is your righteousness (1st Corinthians 1:27-30). The kingdom of God simply means that you are already righteous in Christ and have nothing more to do. You don't have to seek or find the kingdom because God's presence is with you forever. God will provide for all your needs because the kingdom is in you. You already have it.

God is already pleased with you!

We are commanded to keep on believing to attain God's approval. We are told to please God by enduring in faith as written in Hebrews 11:6. But do you know that you are already pleasing to God because Christ lives in you? Do you remember that the Father said that Jesus was His beloved Son in whom He was well pleased in Matthew 3:17? Look at what God the Father says about you!

*Ephesians 1:3-6 NKJV "Blessed be the God and Father of our Lord Jesus Christ, who has **blessed** us with **every** spiritual blessing in the heavenly places in Christ, just as He **chose** us in Him before the foundation of the world, that we should be **holy** and **blameless** before Him in **love**, having **predestined** us to adoption as sons by Jesus Christ to Himself, according to the good **pleasure** of His will, to the praise of the glory of His grace, by which He made us **accepted** in the **Beloved.**"*

Ephesians 1:7-8 NIV "In him we have redemption through his blood, the forgiveness of sins, in accordance with the RICHES of God's GRACE that he LAVISHED on us"

In this most glorious of scriptures, let us feast on the goodness of the Father: It does not say that He will bless us with some blessings if we have faith, but that we were BLESSED with EVERY blessing BEFORE we were even born, or did anything good or bad.
We are not sinners, because He made us HOLY and BLAMELESS, not out of duty but because He LOVED us!
He CHOSE us by grace, and we did not choose Him by our faith.
He PREDESTINED this, and it was not our free will.
The Father ACCEPTED you in the BELOVED (Christ)! You did not accept Him first, because He accepted you before the world began! We only believed the fact that He has always loved us.
He did not do it out of obligation, but with great PLEASURE and happiness! He did not do it stingily, but by LAVISHLY pouring out the RICHES of His GRACE. He did not just give us salvation, but He gave us HIMSELF!

Those under the Law were in the "flesh", that was not pleasing to God because they were trying to be righteous in their own efforts. They were the slaves and servants of the master, trying to earn favor with their performance.

Romans 3:20 "Because by the works of the law, no flesh will be justified in his sight." Romans 8:8-9 "Those who are in the flesh can't please God. But you are not in the flesh but in the Spirit"

But thanks to Jesus, we are not servants, but friends of God and Sons of God! We cannot be in the flesh anymore because the Law has passed away. God is the Father of Christ and our Father too! God does not want employees or servants; He wants you to know that you are His darling son.

John 15:15 "No longer do I call you servants, for the servant doesn't know what his lord does. But I have called you friends, for everything that I heard from my Father, I have made known to you."

John 20:17 "I am ascending to my Father and your Father, to my God and your God."'

The Father is pleased with you because you are His beloved son or daughter through Jesus Christ. God sees no difference between you and Christ because you are one with Him. The Father is pleased because He is pleased with Jesus Christ–not because of your faith or goodness, but because of His LOVE!

God is only interested in your well-being

1st Corinthians 13:5 NIV "Love is not self-seeking"

We have frequently heard that God is doing things against our will, but for His glory. But the truth is that a loving father is not self-seeking because he always wants the glory of His children. When John the Baptist said that he must decrease so that Christ may increase (John 3:30), it did not mean that God wants less of you and more of Him. That verse was talking about the end of John's ministry of the Law so that Christ would now reveal the Grace of God. Today, we live in Christ, and God wants more of you. He wants you to be glorified because your glory is His glory! You are not the clay on the potter's wheel. That was about the Jews being in exile under the Babylonians because they did not keep the Law. You are the finished work, perfect and complete because you are seated with Christ in heavenly places. He does not mold you or break you, but He built you up and made you His beloved Son! In fact, He has already made you perfect in His sight. To say that God wants to "use you" is Old Covenant language. God gives you freedom to express your life with the God-given gifts and dreams that you have! Your life is God's delight. Your dreams are His dreams! God does not want to change you through the circumstances, but He wants you to know that His love is unchanging in all circumstances. We may change, but God's love does not change. God has no expectations from you because you are already perfect! He always has your best interest at heart. He is absolutely selfless, and He displayed this on the cross.

God loves everyone the same

Many believers strongly desire to hear the voice of God. If we don't hear God in an audible voice or have a dream or vision, then we feel inferior thinking that only super-spiritual people experience such bliss. It is not true because God has no favorites. He is a Dad who loves all His kids equally! Now, God speaks in different ways to all of us – but what He says is more important than how He says it. Some people quote Hebrews 4:7 and say that we must always listen to God's warnings and not harden our hearts. They quote Hebrews 12:25 saying that we must hear God's voice otherwise we will face judgment. But the truth is that those scriptures were written to the Hebrew believers who were coming out of the old covenant and were warned to flee the wrath of 70AD when Jerusalem was destroyed. God was telling them to trust in Christ and not be consumed in the judgment of 70AD. It has nothing to do with us. God does not send warnings today, but He only speaks love.

John 10:2-3,8-11 "One who enters in by the door is the shepherd of the sheep. The gatekeeper opens the gate for him, and the sheep listen to his voice .... All who came before me are thieves and robbers, but the sheep didn't listen to them. I am the door. If anyone enters in by me, he will be saved, and will go in and go out, and will find pasture. The thief only comes to steal, kill, and destroy. I came that they may have life, and may have it abundantly. I am the good shepherd. The good shepherd lays down his life for the sheep."

Jesus said that everyone who came before Him were thieves. He was referring to the Pharisees and the old covenant teaching that put heavy religious burdens on the people. Such teachings stole, killed and destroyed the people's lives. Even today, if any religious voice is taking away your peace and joy, it is not from God but man. But the voice of God is the voice of love. Through Jesus Christ, the Father says that He loves you by giving up His life for you. He is not asking you to give anything, but to know that He gave up everything for you. The voice of God is that He loves you. It is not complicated or super-spiritual. If you know that God loves you, then you have heard His voice.

Jeremiah 31:34 "for they shall ALL know me, from their least to their greatest, says God: for I will forgive their iniquity, and their sin will I remember no more"

Everyone will know the Father. This includes the great and small, poor and rich, male and female, old and young. We will all know His love because we are all one with Christ. There are no "men of God" or people with greater anointing. All of us are equally anointed because the anointing is His love for us! We are not "men of God", but we are "sons of the Father". You don't have to be "on fire" for Jesus, because His love for you can never be quenched or reduced, no matter how spiritual you feel. You don't have to come to God through your pastor, priest, prophet, prayer warrior, intercessor, parent, spouse or godfather. It is because He lives in you already and there is no distance between you and Him! You have full access to your Daddy God who loves us as much as He loves Jesus – we are all equally dear to Him.

1st Corinthians 13:2 "I have all faith, so as to remove mountains, but don't have love, I am nothing."

Many believers try to relate to God based on their faith, ministry, service, Church attendance, tithing, moral conduct and other means of performance.

Some believers feel inferior to others who have a lot more Christian pedigree. But the truth is that God loves us passionately even if we don't experience great miracles, speak in tongues, prophesy, know the Bible, lead others or witness to strangers. He loves us even if we struggle in unbelief or have failed in life. No matter who you are or what we do, our Father loves us with all His heart, soul and strength!

God is not serious, but a fun-loving Dad!

Have you been to Christian meetings where the people are relaxed and joking around when they fellowship, but get really serious when they do anything religious? Some try to mourn, fast and cry over their sins because they are trying to be close to God, according to this verse below:

James 4:8-9 "Draw near to God, and he will draw near to you. Cleanse your hands, you sinners; and purify your hearts, you double-minded. Lament, mourn, and weep. Let your laughter be turned to mourning, and your joy to gloom."

But the truth is that James wrote this to the 12 tribes of Israel who were under the great tribulation before the 2nd coming of Christ. He was telling the Jews to stop eating, drinking and partying in Jerusalem because it was going to be destroyed in 70AD. Under the old covenant, there was great fear in God's presence because the Law of Moses imputed sins.

*Hebrews 12:18,21-23 NLT "You have not come to a physical mountain, to a place of flaming fire, darkness, gloom....Moses himself was so frightened at the sight that he said, "I am terrified and trembling." No, you have come to Mount Zion, to the city of the living God, the heavenly Jerusalem, and to countless thousands of angels in a **joyful gathering** ... to the spirits of the **righteous** ones ... who have been made **perfect**"*

But in 70AD, God made a New Covenant where there is great joy and happiness in God's presence because He lives in us and has made us righteous and perfect in the New Jerusalem.

The reason we fear God so much is because we think of Him as a serious old man seated on a distant throne, who needs to be pleased by our faith and actions. God is neither old nor serious. He is called "Ancient of days" because He has no age, without beginning or end! His appearance of "white hair" in the Bible is not because He is old and grumpy, but because it's a symbol of perfect love and wisdom. He is young and vibrant, and He loves you like a little child! God is not serious, but He has great joy and fun with you. In Zephaniah 3:17, God rejoices by singing to you. Just imagine

Him singing to you about how wonderful you are and how much He loves you! He is fun, easy-going and the coolest person we can ever know.

*Luke 15:22-24 "But the father said to his servants, '**Bring out the best** robe, and put it on him. Put a ring on his hand, and shoes on his feet. Bring the fattened calf, kill it, and **let us eat, and celebrate**; for this, my son, was dead, and is alive again. He was lost, and is found.' They began to celebrate ... **music and dancing**"*

He was not stingy, but He gave His best gift to us, by giving up Himself. Remember that He gave up His entire inheritance to the prodigal son. Even after his son wasted all the money, the Father is the one who is lavish in His love, and He celebrates with music and dancing!

Matthew 13:44 "The kingdom of heaven is like treasure hidden in a field. When a man found it, he hid it again, and then in his JOY went and sold ALL he had and bought that field."

When Jesus came to the world, He found all of us and with great joy, He gave up everything in heaven to make us belong to Him! We are the treasure in earthen vessels that Christ purchased by giving up Himself. We are the kingdom of God because Christ died and rose from the dead to live in us!

*Hebrews 12:2 "who for the **JOY** that was set before him endured the cross, despising its shame"*

Jesus went to the cross with great joy because He knew that you would become His brother or sister. He made us holy and sanctified and is proud to say that we are His family.

*Hebrews 2:10-11 "For it became him, for whom are all things, and through whom are all things, in **bringing many children to glory**, to make the author of their salvation perfect through sufferings. For both he who sanctifies and those who are **sanctified** are all from one, for which cause he is not ashamed to call them **brothers**"*

He did not do it half-heartedly. If Jesus went to the cross with such joy, then you can imagine how happy He is with you now that He lives in you!

God is not mad at you. He is madly in love with you!

Alpha and Omega – God's Everlasting Love

During my journey in Christianity, I realized that the greatest indicator of our relationship with God is based on these questions: What do you think of Him: God or Father; Judge or Brother; Boss or Friend? Throughout the Bible, we find that God dealt with man by faith in the Old Creation. But the final revelation of God is love.

1st Corinthians 13:13 "The greatest of these is love."

Are we relating to Him based on our faith or His love? God is LOVE. He does not relate to us based on anything but His love. Unfortunately, religion has created barriers between man and God. But God is not about religion, faith or works. God is only a Father who loves His children. Christians talk about God always in these ways–"we need more faith", "is he pleased with me?", "is this sin?", "we need to do more", "I need to read the Bible more", "I'm not praying much", "I'm not thankful enough". We're always falling short, never doing enough and never being good enough. But God is not looking at our performance. Religion has obstacles and obligations, but God only has open arms of love. Religion is like a contract signed between man and God, in which man is not meeting expectations. But God canceled the contract and wrote your name on His hands and heart! He loves you the way you are because you are His perfect child!

Revelation 21:6 "I am the Alpha and Omega"

He is the Alpha and Omega – which means He is without beginning and end. **God is love, and His love has no beginning or end. There has never been a time when He has not loved us.** We were not even born in the Old Creation or Adam or under the Law. We never had to please Him by faith. We were born as New Creations in Christ as Sons under His love! We were never sinners or enemies of God – those were true for the people under the Law because the Law brought wrath. But the Law passed away, and we are not sinners or servants, but we are SONS. His love is everlasting, and it endures forever. The Father loved you even before you knew Him, even before you knew that Jesus existed or even believed in Him. He loved you before you were born. His love for you is totally one-sided and unconditional. So don't worry about whether He loves you now, because His love never changes. Nothing can change His love for us – not even our struggles of faith or works. The Father's promises and blessings are not dependent on our faith, but on what Jesus did on the cross–which cannot be undone. So then, there is no change in the Father's plans–He cannot stop being good to us and is the same yesterday, today and forever – He is always in love with you.

Nothing can separate us from His love because we are in Christ. You don't need to generate faith to please God. You don't need to convince Him because He is already convincingly in love with you! He was pleased with you before the foundation of the world, and that is why He chose to die for you–to make you His beloved. In Christ, you are always pleasing to the Father. You can never make Him unhappy because it is Christ in you.

Loving one another – Christ fulfilled the Law

When Israel was under the Law, they were commanded to love their neighbor as themselves, but they hated their enemies. But when Christ came, He fulfilled the Law and showed them the true meaning of keeping the Law. He told them that the Law was only fulfilled if they were as perfect as God by loving their enemies. Just when Jesus was about to die on the cross, He gave them a new commandment. He told them to love one another as He loved them. He had given up His life for them on the cross and forgiven even those who crucified Him. At that time, He was commanding them to give up their lives for one another. If they gave up their lives for one another just like Jesus died for them, then they would also be raised from the dead in the resurrection of 70AD. In this way, they would fulfill the Law by following Jesus in persecution and martyrdom (Romans 13:8). If they shrunk back and went to the Old Covenant, then they were judged in 70AD.

To be frank, I don't know anyone who loves others like Jesus. The love we practice is nothing compared to His love. This proves that this commandment was not given to us. It was given only to those under the Law so that they could fulfill the Law by following Jesus in denying themselves and carrying the cross until death. If we were not given the Law, then how can we be asked to fulfill the Law? Christ only gave this commandment to the Jews and not to us, because they were transitioning between the Old to the New Covenant, and therefore He gave them a new commandment. The New Covenant was still not in effect until 70AD. But now after 70AD, we are living under the new covenant where there are no commandments because God's love lives within us, and He causes us to love others without any commandments.

This is true today because there are people in every religion who love each other. We can see Buddhists with integrity and Hindus who accept people of all faiths. Gays and atheists are compassionate to the poor and don't judge others. God is love, and people of all religions, races, sexual orientation, love others because "love" lives in their hearts. Unbelievers display love in spite of not going to Church or learning the Bible. The ironic thing is that Christians can have bad habits and yet still believe in the truth. The point I'm trying to make is that nobody is perfect in his faith or works, but we all have this love for others. This is the New Covenant where God has made ALL of us perfect in Christ. He made us righteous by His perfect love and faith, on our behalf. In the New Covenant, God lives in all humanity because Christ made us righteous by His obedience.

God's original plan of New Covenant Son-ship

We know that Christ made a New Covenant of grace, but this covenant is an everlasting covenant (Jeremiah 32:40, Isaiah 61:8). This means that God's relationship with man as a Father and Son was everlasting. In the beginning, God dealt with Adam as His Father and not His judge. **God never wanted religion, but only sons.** He never told Adam to do anything religious like believing, praying, fasting, tithing, confessing, repenting. He told him to stay away from the knowledge of good and evil – that is defined by moral rules. God did not want Adam to know religion, but to know the Father's love – which is eternal life.

John 17:3 "This is eternal life, that they should know you, the only true God, and him whom you sent, Jesus Christ."

God had created Adam in His image. Adam had no idea about sins, but only knew the Father's love. There was no "faith" at that time, but only love! But Adam sinned, and all humanity became sinners under the Old Covenant Law that came later. The Law was about "do good and avoid evil", and man became conscious of sins and was not aware of the love of the Father. But Christ restored us back as sons. He removed all the guilt and sin-consciousness introduced by religion. He saved us by removing the law and religion, and gave us the knowledge of the Father's loving heart.

Hebrews 8:10 "For this is the covenant that I will make with the house of Israel. After those days," says the Lord; 'I will put my laws into their mind, I will also write them on their heart.'"

You don't need a holy book to teach you how to love, because God is love and He lives within you. Does a father need to take Bible classes on how to love his kids? Do two lovers need training before loving each other? God does not give a list of rules, but His spirit of love flows from within a person who lives in freedom. This love is present in all human beings. If we think of "love" as a commandment from a book or a teacher, then it's just another legalistic rule. It becomes the letter that condemns us when we fail and puffs us up when we succeed. Love is not a commandment, but it is within us. We don't live by rules but by the Spirit or the God-given instinct within us. I see atheists and unbelievers loving others, and they did not learn it in holy books or schools. This is the New Covenant–love is written on our hearts. God is love, and people of all walks, races, religions, sexual orientation, love each other. It is because a book did not teach them, but the God who is love, that lives within all humanity. **Christ has saved us from religion by putting an end to religion and laws that condemn people. He removed religion and brought love to the world.**

Hebrews 8:10 "I will be their God and they will be my people"

God had provided everything to Adam freely. He did not have to earn anything by faith or works. He told Adam to enjoy the free gifts in the garden. He gave him rivers of water (the meaning of the rivers' names is about pleasure). He provided a loving wife (Eve). He provided meaningful work and all of the creation to enjoy. **God was telling Adam, "Just enjoy all I have created for you, my son!"**. At that time, God's presence was with Adam, and he was already His son. But instead, Adam wanted to earn it by knowing good and evil, through his morality. Adam became a servant who had to earn God's blessings by his efforts, and therefore God's presence was not with him anymore. But thanks to Jesus Christ, He has restored us back as sons of God and He lives in us forever.

2nd Corinthians 6:16,18 "For you are a temple of the living God. Even as God said, "I will dwell in them, and walk in them; and I will be their God, and they will be my people." ... I will be to you a Father. You will be to me sons and daughters"

Through Christ, we have now received the Spirit of sons where we know that God is our Father who loves us freely and gives us all things freely.

1st Corinthians 2:12,16 "But we received, not the spirit of the world, but the Spirit which is from God, that we might know the things that were freely given to us by God....we have the MIND of CHRIST"

The people under the Law were the slaves living in fear of God, by having to earn His blessings or be under the curse. They had the spirit of the old covenant world. But we are in the New Covenant as Sons having everything freely provided by our Father. **The mind of Christ means that we have the mindset of sons and not servants.** We know God as Father and not as Judge. You are not the servant on daily wages but the son having the full inheritance because of Christ's finished work. You are not the dog who is eating the crumbs from the master's table, receiving out of his pity. But you are the sons of the Father, feasting from the table being entitled to what already belongs to you! We are sons who have the full inheritance and are far better off than the servants of the old covenant! This is what Adam had before he sinned, and this is what Christ has restored, in the New Covenant. In Ephesians 1:3-4, our Father tells us that He gave us every spiritual blessing in Christ before we were even born. This clearly shows that the New Covenant is everlasting and not based on what we do or believe. It is entirely based on God's unconditional love for us. He is our Father who provides for our lives. At times, we worry about our lives, but He gave us the greatest blessing even before we knew Him.

Psalm 139:16-17 "In your book they were all written, the days that were ordained for me, when as yet there were none of them. How precious to me are your thoughts, God!"

Surely He takes care of our lives because He has ordained it. How precious are His thoughts of love for us! Let us relax and enjoy life with all His free gifts knowing that He loves us. Jesus has finished the work to set us free.

I hope you have enjoyed reading this book. I have definitely enjoyed explaining the love of Jesus to you.

You are accepted in the Father's love, and it's all because of Jesus Christ.

About the author

My name is Mathew Simon. God has blessed me abundantly with a wonderful family. I live with my wife and three children in Northern California. I have been working in Software Engineering since 1996, and by the grace of God, I have been teaching the Bible since 2007.

I also am the author of a Christian Blog that is spreading the Good News of Jesus Christ all over the world: http://goodnews4you.blogspot.com

It is my great desire for you to know that you are accepted in the love of the Father and that you are perfect in Christ.

For questions, comments and feedback, you can contact me by email at mathew.simon@outlook.com

You can also reach me on Facebook at:
https://www.facebook.com/mathew.simon.376

Acknowledgements

I want to thank my ever-loving wife for encouraging me in writing this book. Thank you my beloved darling for your love, prayers and support. I also wanted to especially thank my three wonderful children for their cheerful encouragement. You are the best kids ever! I want to thank my Dad for his love and grace. I want to thank my Mom for her faith and strength. I want to thank my brother, sister and their families, my father-in-law, mother-in-law, brother-in-law and family for their love and prayers. I want to thank all my friends in the Bible-study and prayer groups here in the S.F. Bay Area.

I am especially thankful for the fantastic support of all my friends on Facebook.

I would like to thank the following Bible teachers and ministries:
Joseph Prince http://www.josephprince.org
Andrew Farley https://andrewfarley.org
Simon Yap https://hischarisisenough.wordpress.com
Dr. Chuck Crisco http://anewdaydawning.com
Francis Prabhu Anthony http://www.prabhuantony.org
Tomsan Kattackal https://christiancorrector.blogspot.com
Jonathan Forgor https://enjoyroyalty.wordpress.com
Simeon Edigbe http://reigninglife.blogspot.com
Steve McVey http://www.stevemcvey.com
Paul Ellis https://escapetoreality.org
Sajith Joseph Kottarathil http://sajithjoseph.org
Mar Thoma Church http://marthomasf.org
Don K. Preston http://www.eschatology.org
Adam Maarschalk https://adammaarschalk.com
Grace School of the Bible (Shorewood Bible Church),

V.G. Thomas Kutty (Thiruvalla), Ashish Thomas (Qatar),
David Asomaning, Johny Varghese (Grace India Ministry), Mykael Udy,
Uahamon Austyn, Njoku Henry, Jacob Jakfu,
Ty Cobb, Dan Shaffer, Solomon Muzi Nhlenyama,
Nichole Marbach, & many more.

I want to thank Xulon Inc. for giving me this opportunity.
Above all, I thank God, our Heavenly Father and our Lord Jesus for what He has done for me. It is finished!